THE DISTRICT OF GREENBANK
IN EDINBURGH

THE DISTRICT OF GREENBANK IN EDINBURGH

Malcolm Cant

Preface by

The Rev. Ian G. Scott B.Sc., B.D., S.T.M.

MALCOLM CANT PUBLICATIONS

First published in 1998 by
Malcolm Cant Publications
13 Greenbank Row Edinburgh EH10 5SY

Text copyright © Malcolm Cant
Maps are the copyright of Bryan Ryalls

ISBN 0 9526099 2 4

Typeset and originated by Carnegie Publishing Ltd
Chatsworth Road, Lancaster
Printed and bound by Cromwell Press, Melksham, Wiltshire

To
the people of Greenbank
past, present and future

This First Edition
is limited to .**2000**. *copies*
of which this is
copy number

730
. . . .

Signed by the Author

Contents

Alphabetical List of Subscribers to the First Edition

Adams, L. J.
Adams, R. C. M.
Addison, A. B.
Addison, Stewart
Aglionby, Mrs M.
Aherne, J. F. D.
Aitchison, Ian & Christian
Aitchison, J.
Aitken, Georgina C.
Aldridge, Dr R. D.
Allan, David T. G.
Allan, Elizabeth
Allan, Eric R. & Valerie
Allan, Mr & Mrs J. C.
Allan, Sheriff J. Douglas
Allen, Gina
Allison, Mrs Maureen
Allmark, Frank & Cath
Amara, Nicky
Ambler, Alison & Steve
Amos, Miss M. J.
Anderson, Hamish & Maureen
Anderson, Keith & Sally
Angus, J. G.
Applecross
Archbold, Derek
Armit, Mrs E.
Armit, Jack
Armstrong, N.

Bailey, Noëlle
Bain, Drew
Baines, J.
Baird, Mrs I. A.
Baldwin, John & Vivien

Balfour & Manson, Solicitors
Balfour, Scott
Barclay, Andrew W.
Barclay, David
Barclay, Joseph T. & Georgina H.
Barclay, Mr & Mrs W. A.
Barr, Peter W.
Barraclough, Christine & David
Barrie, Joyce M.
Barron, Dr & Mrs B. D.
Bayram, M. C.
Beards, Diane & Paul
Beaumont, Mark
Beeby, J. K.
Bell, Mrs Jean W.
Bell, Julia
Bell, Margaret D.
Bell, Mr & Mrs T. W.
Bennet, James A.
Berkley, Mrs J. G.
Berkley, Keith J.
Berrie, J. E.
Berrill, Maurice
Bertram, Alice
Bertram, Sheila
Birrell, Dave
Black, Charles & Susan
Black, J. C.
Black, Dr Neil
Blackhall, Winifred (née Addison)
Blackie, Dorothy & Michael
Blair, Mary B.
Bland, Roger & Diana
Boa, Mrs Esther
Bonaly Primary School

Bond, Dr S. B.
Borthwick, Alan
Boyd, Chris
Boyd, Marie
Bradford, Mrs D.
Bradshaw, A. R.
Brebner, M. J.
Bridges, Alan & Brenda
Brockie, Canon Bill
Brotchie, Alan W.
Brotherston, Kate
Brough, Alex
Brown, Allan and Gray, Alison
Brown, Mrs A. S.
Brown, Carol
Brown, Miss E. R.
Brown, Ernest W.
Brown, Fergus J. M., W.S.
Brown, Isobel & Eric
Brown, J. M. & Mrs E. M.
Brown, K. G.
Brown, Mrs P. E.
Brown, William A.
Brownlee, Fiona
Bruce, J. S. & E. J.
Buchan, Catherine Charlotte
Buchan, Hazel & Ian
Bulmer, Sheila H. (née Stewart)
Burges, Wendy
Burnet, Mrs G. W.
Burnie, Mr & Mrs Andrew G.
Burnie, Mrs Elsie W.
Butchart, Elizabeth

Cairns, Alistair
Cairns, Joan L.
Cameron, Alan & Alison
Cameron, C. N.
Cameron, Mrs Isobel
Cameron, James M.
Campbell, Colin
Campbell, Jessie & Archie
Campbell, M. S.
Cant, Graham & Denise
Cant, Phyllis M.

Carbarns, Douglas M.
Carmichael, Dr Peter, C.B.E., B.Sc.
and surviving grandchildren of
   Henry Carmichael:
    Adams, Anne McDonald
    Barter, Effie Carmichael
    Hope, Helen Gillies
    McGhie, Mary
    Palmer, Catherine
    Robertson, John Carmichael
    Short, John Hendry
    Short, Raymond
    Strachan, Alastair Carmichael
    Wright, Christina McLaren
Carnegie, Mr & Mrs William
Carpenter, Sarah
Carter, Mr & Mrs J.
Cato, Irene (née Somerville)
Caw, David
Chalmers, Elizabeth
Chalmers, John
Chalmers, Mr & Mrs W. P.
Chantler, Linda, Iain & Gillian
Chapman, Emma
Chapman, Dr Ian David
Cheetham, Ben
Chittleburgh, Nicola & Jeremy
Christie, Mr & Mrs J. B.
Christie, Marion
Clark, Mrs Doreen
Clark, Mrs G.
Clark, June
Clark, Mrs J. K.
Clark, Margaret & Gerrard
Clark, Stanley H.
Clarke, Mrs M.
Clarkson, T. W.
Clement, Mrs A. W.
Clunie, William
Clyde, Mrs Caroline
Cockburn, George A. & Doreen
Coghill, Hamish & Mary
Collin, Norman
Collins, Mrs Margaret
Comiston Primary School

Common, Lynne
Constable, G. G.
Cook, A. M.
Cook, Mr & Mrs David D.
Cook, Helen & Cyril
Cooke, Marwyn & John
Cormack, A. K.
Corsie, George L.
Costello, M. & F.
Costello, Seán
Coutts, Mr & Mrs D. F.
Coventry, Mr & Mrs A.
Cowell, E. S.
Cowper, A. S.
Cowper, Charlie & Rosemary
Crabb, Ronald S.
Craig, Mr & Mrs J. N.
Craig, Mrs Mavis
Crainer, George
Cramond, R. D., C.B.E.
Cremona, Dr A.
Crichton, Mrs I. K.
Crichton, Mrs Isobel K.
Croal, Joan Elizabeth
Crosbie, T. R.
Crosby, Pat & Walter
Cruickshank, Graeme D. R.
Cumming, Mrs L.
Cunningham, Mrs E. M.
Cunyngham-Brown, James
Cuthbertson, Ian & Faye
Czemerys, Michael & Annette

Dale, Colin
Daly, Mrs M.
Darwell-Stone, Julian & Eleanor
Davidson, Daniel & Maida
Davidson, Elizabeth M.
Davidson, John M.
Davidson, Thomas L.
Davies, Armin John
Davies, Brenda Nicol
Davies, D. Leighton
Davis, Brian & Lesley
Dawson, Katie & Emma

Deas, A. J.
Deeley, Pamela J.
Dewar, Ross
Dick, Susan M.
Dickie, Mr & Mrs C. P.
Didcock, Ernest
Dignan, John
Dobbie, Rosemary
Doig, Andrew
Donaldson, Elizabeth
Donaldson, Robert
Douglas, Alison M.
Douglas, Gavin
Douglas, Margaret S.
Douglas, Mr & Mrs N. F.
Duffus, John & Hazel
Duffy, Mrs Sheila
Dumble, Mrs Frances (née Laing)
Dunbar, Richard & Julia
Dunlop, Alastair
Dunn, Fenella
Durie, Muriel (née Addison)
Duvall, Dr & Mrs E.
Dyble, Keith

Eckstein, Evelyn
Edinburgh City Archives
Edinburgh City Libraries
Edwards, Darby
Elder, J. S.
Elgin, Mrs Muriel
Elliot, Dora & George
Elliot, Mrs G. B.
Ellis, Alan & Amelia
Ellis, Bill & Pat
Everett, Mrs J. M.
Everett, Kirstin & John

Faed, Stuart & Caroline
Fairley, Mr & Mrs R. I.
Falconer, Miss M.
Fantes, Peter
Farmer, Sir Tom, C.B.E.
Fentiman, Alan H. B.
Fenton, Professor Alexander

Ferguson, Mr & Mrs I. T.
Ferguson, J. P. S.
Ferguson, Patrick
Ferguson, Mrs Roy
Fiddes, Mrs D. O.
Fielding, Mrs Ann
Fincham, John R. S.
Finlay, Mr & Mrs R. A. L.
Finlayson, Calum D. C.
Finlayson, Helen M.
Finnie, Jean & George
Fisher, Mrs E. M.
Fisk, Flora & Peter
Fletcher, Alan
Flynn, Brian
Flynn, Jane
Fontana, Mr & Mrs J.
Forbes, Mr & Mrs M.
Forrest, Jill
Forrest, Mr & Mrs Matthew
Foster, Martin
Foster, Tony & Liz
Fraser, George U.
Fraser, Malcolm & Trish
Fraser, Margo & Bill

Gallacher, Mark
Gallacher, Trudi
Galloway, Louise
Garden, Mrs Doris
Gardiner, Mrs Annie B.
Gardner, Janette
Gardner, Kathleen
Geddes, William G.
Gellatly, Dilys
Gelly, James D.
Gelly, J. L.
George, Jane
Gibb, J. Jeffrey
Gibson, Dave & Jean
Gibson, Moira
Gilchrist, Iain M.
Giles, Don & Hilary
Gilliatt, Alison J.
Gilliatt, John S.

Gillies, Angela M. & Iain G. L.
Girdwood, Professor & Mrs R. H.
Girdwood, Mr & Mrs R. S. H.
Glen, Catherine F.
Glendinning, Doris & Peter
Glendinning, Mrs M.
Glennie, Brian
Goddard, Ian
Goldsbrough, Margaret
Goodall, Mrs Margaret
Goodlet, Mr & Mrs W. E.
Gordon, Alan & Nancy
Goudy, R. G.
Gould, Ingrid & Douglas
Gould, John & Frances
Graham, Ian R.
Graham, Peter & Isabel
Grahame, E. A.
Grant, Alan G.
Gray, Dr James A.
Gray, N. D. & J. S.
Gray, Miss O.
Gray, Rosemary D.
Greenbank Parish Church Archives
Greening, Professor & Mrs John
Greenshields, Mrs C.
Grenfell, Helen
Griffiths, Derek & Beryl
Griffiths, Keith and Smart, Fiona
Grouchy, Philip M. L. de
Guerin, Paul & June
Guild, S. A.
Gunn, Alastair G.

Hagart, Maureen & Ian
Haggart, Margaret
Haggerty, James
Haggerty, William
Hairs, H. C.
Hall, James A.
Halliday, Mr & Mrs D.
Hannan, R.
Harley, Jack
Harper, Rev. Donald D. H.
Harper, Mr & Mrs R. C. M.

Harrod, Martin & Sharon
Harwell, George G.
Harwell, Mrs V. N.
Haston, J.
Hay, Miss Mary M. D.
Henderson, Bob & Charlotte
Hennigan, William
Hepburn, Alexander I.
Heptonstall, Mary & Barrie
Herd, W. M. (New Zealand)
Hilton, Calum
Hilton, Christopher
Hilton, Susanna
Hilton, Jo
Historic Scotland
Hoffie, William A.
Hogg, Douglas
Hogg, Mrs J.
Hogg, T. A. J.
Holmes, Fran
Hood, Mrs E. D.
Hood, James H.
Horberry, Eric
Horn, M. E.
Horne, Mrs Barbara
Horne, Mr & Mrs John A.
Hosack, Iain & Maisie
Hughes, Alastair
Hughes, Barry & Helen
Hughes, Ceri
Hughes, Duncan
Hughes, Mr & Mrs James
Hume, E. A.
Hume, M.
Hunt, John M.
Hunter, Bill & Anne
Hunter, George R.
Hunter, Ian
Hunter, Lyn & Maurice
Hunter, Richard
Hunter, Mr & Mrs W. M. M.
Hunter's Tryst Primary School
Husband, Charles & Lorna
Hutcheson, James

Illingworth, Dr Stephen
Imlach, Michael
Inch, Jim
Inch, Susan
Inchley, Dr & Mrs C. J.
Ingham, Kathleen
Ingram, Margaret
Innes, Dr Elizabeth
Innes, Dr James
Innes, Nicki & David
Ireland, R. D.
Isles, Ian & Betty

Jackson, Diana Barbara
Jackson, Mrs J.
Jackson, N. M.
James, H. J. & B. R.
Jamieson, Mrs E. F.
Jardine, Roy
Jenkins, Mrs L.
Johnson, Keith & Connie
Johnson, Robert & Joan
Johnston, Ms. C.
Johnston, Keith
Johnston, Very Rev. Dr W. B.
Johnstone, Mr & Mrs J. G. J.
Johnstone, Tom
Jurgenson, C. J.

Keane, Jarlath & Alice
Kelly, Bill & Jacqui
Keppie, James
Kerr, A. M.
Kerr, Colin
Kettles, Mrs Tricia
Kidd, William H.
King, Donald
King, Mr & Mrs D. F.
King, Lorraine
King, Rachel
King, Robert
Kinnear, Anne & Ewen
Kinnear, Helen & Jennifer
Kinnear, Robert Ian
Kirton-Vaughan, Alex

Kotowska, K. M.

Laidlaw, Christine
Laing, Eric T.
Laing, L. B.
Land, Ray
Lavin, Jim & Sheila
Law, Colin & Kirsty
Lean, Dan & Alison
Leitch, A. & E.
Leitch, Laura
Levinson, Victor
Lindley, Harry G.
Lockerbie, Allan & Linda
Logan, Lt. Col. J. F.
Logie, Miss Sheila
Lonie, Mrs C. G.
Lonie, James G.
Lorimer, Lindsay
Low, John
Lowden, Jean
Lowe, David
Lowe, Margaret
Lucas, E. M.
Lugton, Jim
Lumsdaine, Colin
Lumsdaine, Craig
Lumsdaine, Eleanor
Lumsdaine, Scott
Lumsden, Mrs H.
Lyddon, C
Lyon, Mr & Mrs E. J.
Lyon, Mr & Mrs K. J.
Lyster, Mrs Margaret

McAnsh, W. D.
McBain, David
McBean, Scott
McCalden, Eric
McCall, Roddick
McCartney, Moira S. F.
McClean, T. J.
MacCormick, Flora & Neil
McCulloch, Robert
McCurrach, Ewan

McCurrach, Katy
MacDonald, Alistair Young
McDonald, Mrs B.
MacDonald, Colin
Macdonald, Duncan & Christine
MacDonald, E. Jane
McDonald, Fiona
MacDonald, Ian
Macdonald, John C.
Macdonald, M.
Macdonald, Dr Morag M.
McDougall, S.
McDougall, Drs S.R. & H., and
    Lewis
McEwan, James D.
McGuigan, David
McGuire, G.
McIlwrick, Elizabeth M.
McIlwrick, Eric B.
McIlwrick, Gilbert Maurice
McIntosh, D. R. & S. J.
McIntyre, Mr & Mrs Andrew
McIvor, Brian & Maureen
Mackay, Elizabeth
Mackay, The Family of Donald &
    Peggy
Mackay, H. & D.
Mackay, Sheila M.
MacKay, Mr & Mrs W. G. S.
McKendrick, Mrs A. D.
Mackenzie, Mrs Elizabeth C.
Mackenzie, Pat
Mackinlay, Alan L.
Mackinlay, Jean
Mackinnon, Aileen D.
MacKinnon, Eilidh
MacKinnon, Euan
MacKinnon, Hamish
McLaughlin, John
Maclean, Dr Una
Macleod, Robert R. & Pat
McMahon, Dr Mary R.
McMaster, Mrs Moira
McMichael, Christina
Macmillan, D. C.

McMinn, J. S.
McMurran, Christine
Macneil and Mrs Macneil of Barra
Macniven, Duncan & Valerie
McPake, Mr & Mrs A. M.
McQuillan, Miss Elaine M.
McQuillan, Dr Ruth
Macrae, Mr & Mrs Kenneth D.
McWilliam, Dr Joan
Maguire, John
Mair, Mrs S.
Malone, Cathy, John, Amy &
    Martin
Mannings, Mike
Manson, Mrs Diana M.
Manson, Laura J. E.
Marlow, John F.
Marryatt, Mrs H. M.
Marshall, Andrew
Marshall, Mrs James I. H.
Marshall, Miss M.
Marshall, Mrs S. M.
Martin, A. S.
Martin, Tom
Martin, Tom L.
Martin, W. W.
Martin, William & Pauline
Mason, Pamela
Masterton, Joyce & Jim
Mavor, Tom & Ella
May, Dr & Mrs F.
May, G.
Mayer, Victoria
Mearns, Mr & Mrs Hamish
Meiklejohn, Jennifer
Melrose, Michael & Susan
Melville, Professor Ian
Menzies, Mr & Mrs A. I.
Merritt, Jon
Middleton, Iain
Millar, Dr Paul
Millar, Robert R.
Miller, Ann & Catrine
Milligan, Nancy & Gordon
Milliken, Mrs W. Alastair

Milne, J. & M.
Milne, Winnie & Harley
Mimpriss, Mrs E. J.
Mitchell, Mrs A. C.
Mitchell, Ian
Moffat, Mrs Jean
Monro, Anita
Moonie, A. G.
Morrison, Bryce
Morrow, Alex & Christina
Moss, Heather
Moussa, Dr S. A.
Mowatt, Mrs M. P.
Moyes, Robert
Mullen, Mrs M.
Munro, Rev. G. A. M.
Munro, Mr & Mrs J.
Munro, Jennifer M.
Munro, Mr & Mrs R. W.
Murphy, Mrs Eileen E.
Murphy, M.
Murray, Mrs Ethel
Mutch, Chivas & Joyce
Myddleton, Mrs Maureen
Myles, Pete & Katie

Napier, Charles
Napier University Library
Nelson, Jessie M.
Nicholson, Mr & Mrs D. F.
Nicholson, Mr & Mrs I.
Nicholson, Jean
Nimmo, Elaine
Nimmo, Julie & Robin
Noble, Miss J. D.
Noble, Mrs Norma E.

O'Brien, Joanna Margaret Louise
O'Brien, Karen & John
O'Brien, Kathryn Melissa
Ogilvie, A. T. F.
Oldroyd, Brenda E.
Oliver, Alexandra
Oliver, Catherine
Oliver, Chris

Osborne, Mrs H. C.
O'Sullivan, Mike
Oxbrow, Anne

Parker, D. H.
Paterson, Alex
Paterson, Irene & Bobby
Paterson, Jim
Paterson, John
Paterson, M.
Patrick, Miss Kathleen M.
Paul, Gillian
Pentland, Mrs Sandra
Pentland Review Local Community
    Newspaper
Perry, Jeanette
Peterson, A. M.
Philip, Mrs E. M.
Philip, Dr G. P.
Phillips-Dutot, Gladys
Picken, Eliot
Picken, Helen & Jim
Pirie, Athol J.
Pirnie, Rodger
Pitkeathly, Ian & Margaret
Polley, J.
Porteous, Cliff & Libby
Pottinger, Mary
Pryde, Brian

Raemaekers, Patricia & Jeremy
Ramsay, Margaret
Rankin, Captain & Mrs Robert
Rankine, W. K. & S. H.
Reaper, Mrs Jean
Reid, David & Alison
Reid, D. M.
Reid, Elizabeth
Reid, John & Margot
Reid, Robin
Rendall, John F.
Reynolds, Mr & Mrs R.
Richardson, Judith
Richardson, William M. P.
Riddell, Colin

Rigg, Trevor & Anne
Rimer, David
Ritchie, George
Ritchie, Jean
Ritchie, John D.
Robb, Mr & Mrs George
Roberts, Iona
Robertson, A. A.
Robinson, D. A.
Robinson, George
Robinson, Ian
Robinson, Michael
Robinson, William G.
Ronald, Chris & Catriona
Roper, Michael James
Rose, Mrs Alison
Rosie, Graham
Ross, A. & E.
Ross, David T.
Rossi, John Duncan
Rowand, Mr & Mrs Donald M.
Royal Commission on the Ancient
and Historical Monuments of
    Scotland
Royal Scottish Academy
Rushbrook, Mrs A. H.
Russell, David
Russell, Mrs H. A.
Russell, Peter
Russell, Robert S.
Rutherford, John
Ryalls, Bryan & Jenni
Ryalls, Kevin & Sandra
Ryalls, Niall

Sanders, Andrew
Sanders, Duncan
Sanders, Sarah
Sanders, Stuart & Barbara
Sangster, Graeme
Saunders, Helen W.
Saunders, Mr & Mrs J. K.
Sclare, Goldwyn & Muriel
Scott, Miss Frances A.
Scott, Rev. Ian G.

Scott, Mrs Jean (née Macpherson)
Scott, John H.
Scott, Linda A.
Scott, M.
Scott, Tom
Scoular, Patricia
Sheen, Mr & Mrs K.
Shelbourn, Kathy
Shepherd, Dr W. C.
Sibbald, Mr & Mrs R.
Siller, Ann & Martin
Siller, Colin
Siller, Morag
Simpson, Alan & Sue
Simpson & Brown, Architects
Simpson, Effie S. (née Warwick)
Simpson, James A.
Sinclair, Donald
Skedd, Edward
Skilling, J.
Small, A.
Small, D.
Small, F.
Small, John P.
Small, Moira
Small, S.
Smith, Mrs Alice
Smith, Andrew, Lesley, Cameron &
   Tara
Smith, Mrs Catherine
Smith, Charles J., Hon.B.Sc.
Smith, David & Dianne
Smith, Doris
Smith, Rev. J. A. Wemyss, M.A.
Smith, Joan
Smith, Kirsty C. Lupton
Smith, Robert Lupton, O.B.E.
Smith, Mrs Sheila
Smith, Mrs S.B.
Smith, W. R., B.Sc.
Sneddon, Mary (née Cant)
Soden, Joanna
South Morningside Primary School
Spence, Mr & Mrs J. H.
Squire, J. & P.

Steedman, John G.
Steedman, June L.
Stein, Robert C.
Stephen, Harry
Stevenson, Mrs Helen
Stevenson, Moira
Stevenson, Randall
Stevenson-Renwick Family
Stewart, Mrs A.
Stewart, Ann
Stewart, Douglas F.
Stewart, Gordon
Stewart, Iain & Ros
Stewart, John
Stewart, Mrs M.
Stewart, Morag J.
Still, D.
Stillwell, Mrs B. A.
Stimpson, Fiona & Robin
Strachan, M.
Strang, Elspet A. G.
Styles, Mrs E. M.
Sutherland, Derek & Irene
Sutherland, Margaret & Rab
Sutton, Mark and Branding, Antje
Swann, Mr & Mrs A. M.

Taylor, Mrs C.
Taylor, Dave
Tetlaw, Paul
Thin, James, Ltd.
Thom, Isobel
Thomson, Colin
Thomson F. & E. & N.
Thomson, G. L.
Thomson, J.
Thwaites, C. E.
Thwaites, D. I.
Timmons, R. Bryan
Tod, Vivienne
Todd, Mr & Mrs W.
Torrance, Thomas S.
Tough, Derek M.
Train, Alexandra E.
Train, Raymond

Preface

Some years ago I received a copy of David Dorward's book *Scotland's Place-names*. Immediately I turned to the name Kirkcaldy, my home town. I have not lived there for almost thirty years and I no longer have any family connection with the town. Even my school companions are scattered far and wide. But it is the place of my roots and, as such, it has, and always will have, a special significance for me. I next looked up Edinburgh, my adopted home, which holds a special place in my heart. I mention this because I am convinced that the places of our lives have much to do with who and what we are. Indeed Dr Paul Tournier, the medical practitioner of Geneva who was also a theologian and prolific author, writes: 'Man is not a pure spirit, and he has part in the places in which he has lived and experienced joy or sadness. He is bound up with matter, with things, with the ground he lives on. Our place is our link with the world. All the places we have lived in remain with us, like the pegs in a vast storehouse, on which our memories are hung'.

What might seem to be no more than a broad general interest in the places we inhabit may thus turn out to be much more. It represents some degree of search for identity. We want to know the stories of the homes we live in and the streets we walk and the public buildings around us, for these contribute to our story and will contribute to our children's stories. Similarly, when we visit a strange town, on holiday say, we try to find out as much as we can about its places of interest and its history, for thus we acquire a deeper understanding of the place and its people. Even a brief visit may feed into our treasure house of memories.

In his growing series of books about Edinburgh and its various parts Malcolm Cant by his painstaking research puts into our hands reliable facts about the places of our lives, whether we live in them or simply visit them. Having lived in Greenbank for the past fifteen years and worked closely as a parish Minister with so many of its folk and its institutions, I welcome his latest production about this part of the city that is so closely related to, yet distinctively different from, the Morningside out of which it grew as one of Edinburgh's more recent suburbs.

Here we find in eminently readable form the story of the farm on the road south and we learn of the development of the spreading city. Residents and visitors alike will find much here to intrigue and will be inspired to walk the now familiar streets and compare text and photographs to trace that development for themselves.

The book's appearance is timely, for the author has been able to use not only archive documentation but also the oral tradition of those who have clear memories of some of the events he records. It is timely for another reason, however, for the Greenbank area is in the midst of significant change with the earlier closure of Greenlea and the impending closure of the City Hospital, two institutions that played a significant part in the pioneering growth of the district and to a large extent contributed to its character. New housing that replaces these will move Greenbank on to another phase of growth and the consequences of growth.

I am delighted to have this privilege of commending Malcolm Cant's book and thanking him for a helpful and informative guide to this district which has played such an important part in my life and has contributed so much to the city of Edinburgh.

The Rev. Ian G. Scott B.Sc., B.D., S.T.M.
Minister of Greenbank Parish Church

Introduction and Acknowledgments

I first visited Greenbank around 1950 when I was a young pupil at James Gillespie's Boys' School in Marchmont Crescent. A friend and I accepted a dare to follow the teacher home, which meant that we had to board the No. 9 bus in Marchmont Crescent at the same time as the teacher, Miss Gray. We had no idea where we were going, but the bus took a meandering route through the districts of Grange, Blackford and Morningside, before apparently heading for the Pentland Hills at the top of Morningside Drive. To us, this was the country. The route took us up Greenbank Lane and Greenbank Road to the corner of Greenbank Row where the bus reversed into the opening, ready for the return journey. We were completely confused by this and lost sight of our original objective. Much to our embarrassment, Miss Gray came up to us and asked why we were so far from home. She escorted us down Greenbank Road to Braidburn Valley Park and left us with strict instructions that we were to return to the bus terminus before dark. Before leaving us, she checked that we had our bus fare home, but we never really discovered where she lived. However, many years later, when my wife and our family came to live at Greenbank Row, lo and behold, Miss Gray was living in the house opposite. Frequently, she would chat to me about my early school days but she never made reference to my first, or subsequent, visits to Greenbank. In later life, some people regard their teachers as rather distant characters. I can honestly say that I never found Miss Gray to be distant – possibly because I was never any further away from her than the second front seat! If she were alive today, I don't know what she would make of this acknowledgment, or of what lies ahead in the following pages, but, hopefully, she might have enjoyed it.

I need to thank a great number of people other than Miss Gray. If anything, this book has involved an even larger group of people than some of my other studies. The simplest method is for me to mention, firstly, the various libraries and repositories of information relevant to the book. These include the Cockburn Association; the Edinburgh City Archivist's Department; the Edinburgh Room of the Edinburgh Central Library; Edinburgh University Library; the Imperial War Museum; the Merchants of Edinburgh Golf Club; Napier University; the National Library of Scotland; the Old Edinburgh Club; the Royal Commission on the Ancient and Historical Monuments of Scotland; the Royal Incorporation of Architects in Scotland; the Royal Institute of British Architects; the Royal Scottish Academy; the Saltire Society; The Scotsman Publications Limited; the Scottish Record Office; Sotheby's Picture Library; South Morningside Primary School; and West Lothian Council Libraries.

At an early stage in my research, records were made available to me through the Trotter family of Charterhall, and Mrs Brenda L. Rennie of Balfour & Manson, Solicitors in Edinburgh. Several descendants of the building contractors were most helpful in putting together the story of the Hepburns, the Robinsons and the Keppies. Slightly more elusive was the story of the builder, Theodore K. Irvine, which was eventually tracked down with the assistance of John Chalmers, Mrs A. H. Rushbrook and West Lothian Libraries. Other specific areas of assistance were: Miller Homes: Fraser S. Conn, Ramsay Tubb and Alex Paterson; Mortonhall Tennis Club: Mrs Isobel Thom, Miss Margaret Bell and Miss M. J. Brebner; Southern Light Opera Company: David McBain, Mrs Doris Garden and Neville Garden; Gordon Wright, who published *The Place Names of Edinburgh*; and the Braid Hills Hotel: John C. Dignan, General Manager. The section on the City Hospital was put together with a great deal of assistance from Dr James A. Gray, who is in the course of writing a full history of the hospital.

I also conducted a large number of interviews with people whose collective knowledge of Greenbank enabled me to add much of the flesh to the bones. Their contribution was invaluable, but the list is lengthy: Mr & Mrs Adam, Mrs Addie, Mrs Aitken, Mrs E. Armit, Mrs Noelle Bailey, Mrs Boa, Mrs Sheila Bulmer, Jessie & Archie Campbell, Dr Peter Carmichael, John & Elizabeth Chalmers, William Clunie, Mr & Mrs Coventry, Mrs Cunningham, Mrs M. E. Elgin, R. I. Fairley, Mrs Pat Ferguson, Martin Foster, William G. Geddes, Mrs Gellatly, Catherine Glen, Mrs Frances Gould, Jennie Harper, George G. Harwell, W. Hoffie, Mr & Mrs Horne, Eddie Hume, Ann & Bill Hunter, Mr & Mrs Johnstone, Sheila Logie, Moira McCartney, Mr & Mrs Macdonald,

David McGuigan, Elizabeth McIlwrick, Eric McIlwrick, Miss E. McQuillan, Miss Ruth McQuillan, Tom Martin, Mr & Mrs Masterton, Ian Melville, Dr Paul Millar, Ian Mitchell, Moggie family descendants, Mrs Paterson, Mrs Jeanette Perry, Athol Pirie, Bill Robinson, Derek Robinson, Chris Ronald, Frances A. Scott, John Scott, Bill Smith, Charles J. Smith, Mrs Freda Sneddon, Douglas Still, Paul Tetlaw, Mrs Vivien Tod, Miss Margaret Tullis, Councillor J.L. Walls, Marjorie Watson, Robert Watson, Miss W. Watson, Mrs E. Whyte, Miss Isla Wilkie, and Miss Harvey Wood.

Many people also lent photographs, several of which are included in the following pages, with due acknowledgment. I am particularly indebted to Mrs Pat Mackenzie of South Morningside Primary School for the photograph, on the back cover, of pupils who were involved in the school's centenary celebrations in 1992. The maps at the beginning of the book were again completed for me by the able pen of Bryan Ryalls. The Sanders family enthusiastically undertook the distribution of publicity material, firstly, when I was looking for information, and later when I was looking for subscribers. An excellent response was received for which I thank you all.

Neville Moir handled production, Jim Hutcheson undertook design, and John and Val Tuckwell dealt with all editorial work and proof-reading.

My particular thanks go to the Rev. Ian G. Scott, Minister of Greenbank Parish Church for writing the Preface and for his interest throughout the project; also to the members of the Kirk Session, and to Graham Rosie, the archivist.

Finally, I thank my wife Phyllis and our extended family for their support in this ever-pervasive pastime of mine. When I first started to write about Edinburgh several years ago our own family had sufficient time to undertake all sorts of tasks for me. They still do but shortly I shall need to look to the grandchildren for continuity.

I hope you enjoy, and reflect on, *The District of Greenbank in Edinburgh* in the same way as I have done during a long association with the district.

Malcolm Cant F.C.I.I., F.S.A.(Scot.)

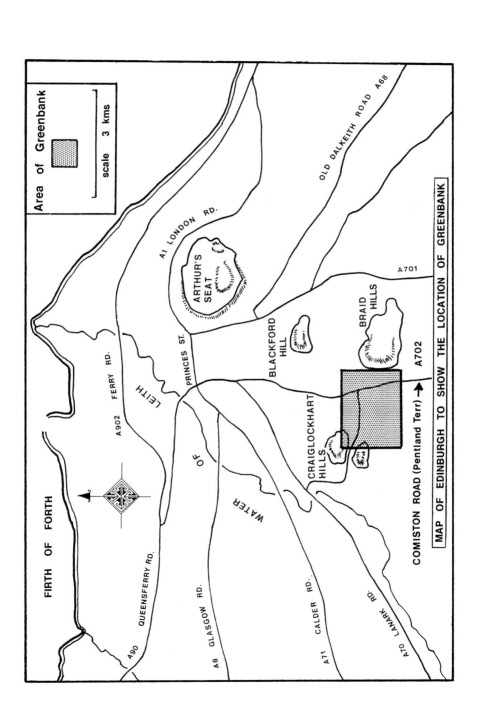

MAP OF EDINBURGH TO SHOW THE LOCATION OF GREENBANK

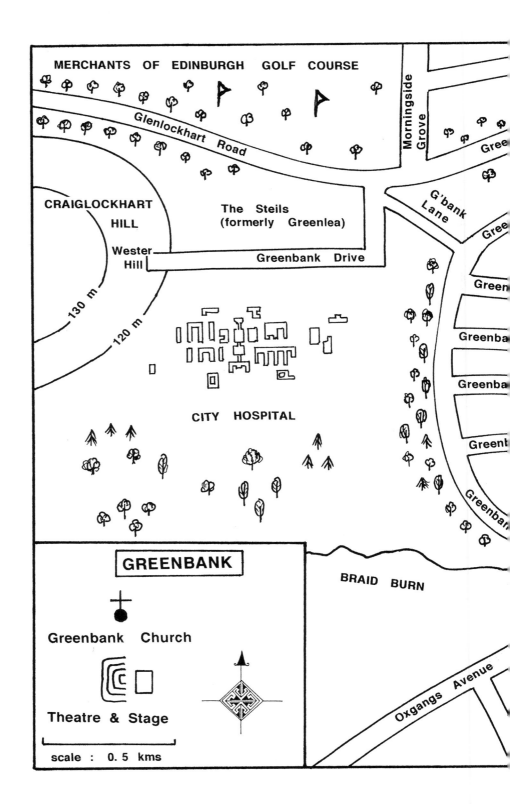

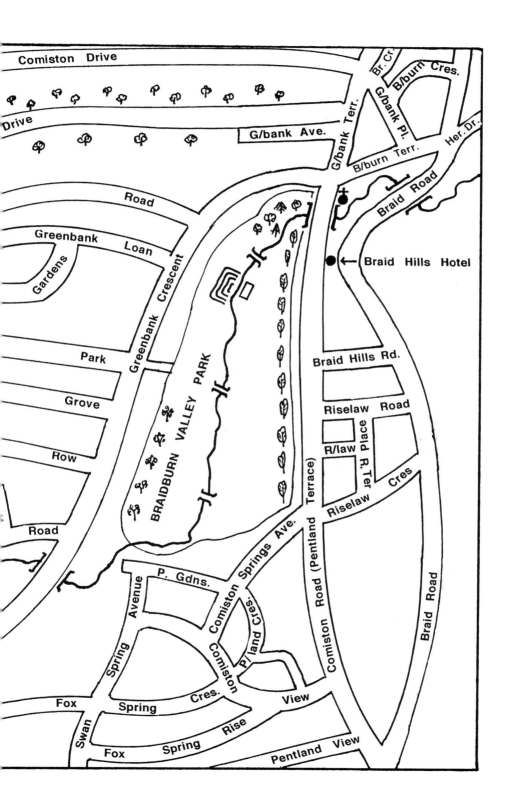

The History and Development of Greenbank and its Environs

The name 'Greenbank' probably came to prominence as a separate district of Edinburgh in the 1930s when the remaining fields of Greenbank Farm succumbed to bungalow development. The name, which has a purely descriptive derivation, can, however, be traced to at least the early seventeenth century, as an alternative name for Over Plewlands of Braid. Its original boundaries are still evident, although obscured by subsequent road and housing developments. The original Lands of Greenbank covered a much wider area than the modern district of Greenbank. Starting at the east end of Braidburn Terrace, the boundary ran southwards along the line of Braid Road to the Buck Stone, which marked the junction of four estates: Comiston, Greenbank, Braid and Mortonhall. From there it ran with the Comiston boundary by the south end of Braidburn Valley Park. The western march is more definite – along the line of the back gardens on the west side of Greenbank Road, where they abut onto the grounds of the City Hospital. Finally, the northern boundary ran along the line of the small burn hidden by trees on the north side of Greenbank Drive, and hence back to the starting point, via Greenbank Place. Within that area the most substantial buildings were Greenbank farmhouse and steadings, positioned on the west side of the arable farmland, now occupied by the east corner of Greenbank Loan and Greenbank Gardens. The traditional approach to Greenbank Farm was from Braid Road along the line of the first Greenbank Road, which was later widened and developed as Braidburn Terrace. It was not until about 1830 that the old Braid Road to Penicuik and Biggar was superseded by a new thoroughfare, later named Comiston Road and Pentland Terrace. *Gellatly's New Map of the Country 12 Miles Round Edinburgh,* dated 1836, clearly shows the long straight sections of the new road in contrast to the awkward bends and gradients of Braid Road. The same map shows the neighbouring farms of Comiston, Oxgangs, Colinton Mains, Craiglockhart, Braid and Morton Hall, the home of the Trotter family who owned the Lands of

Greenbank. The new road effectively cut Greenbank into two sections, precipitating its eventual demise as a rural community.

Although the 1830 road cut the estate in two, it was not immediately followed by further building. The *Ordnance Survey Map*, 1851, shows no building work south of the tollhouse, which stood near the site of the present Post Office in Morningside Road. The first structure of any size was the City Poorhouse on Glenlockhart Road which was opened in 1870. Even by 1882 there were no tenement buildings shown on Comiston Road. The few Greenbank addresses which existed were given a postal address 'Lothianburn' until about 1890. In the 1880s houses were under construction in the section bounded by Braid Crescent, Braid Road, Braidburn Terrace and Greenbank Terrace, and the Braid Hills Hotel had been designed but not yet completed. By 1900 the first Greenbank Church had been built, shortly after the high-level section of Pentland Terrace. The houses of Riselaw were built progressively between 1897 and 1937.

The 1891 *Census* gives some idea of the indigenous population living at Greenbank towards the end of the nineteenth century. At Braidburn Dairy (at the north end of Mortonhall Tennis Club courts) William Mitchell lived with his wife Grace and their two daughters and one son, along with Mary Sterrat, the dairymaid, and Robert Jackson, a farm

Curling Pond Cottage, or Braidburn Cottage, *c.* 1913. The building was used from around 1890 in connection with Morton Hall Curling Club and then by Mortonhall Tennis Club until it was demolished in 1957.

The first Greenbank United Presbyterian Church was opened in Braidburn Terrace in 1900 and is now used as the halls of Greenbank Parish Church. Curling Pond Cottage can be seen to the left of the church. The picture is dated after 1900 but before 1906 when the south side of Braidburn Terrace was built. *Courtesy of Greenbank Parish Church.*

servant. Within a few hundred yards was Morton Hall Curling Club Pond House where Robert Ferguson, a master slater, lived with his wife Isabella and their three daughters and one son. At Greenbank Farm six separate households are listed under the names Henderson, Lawrie, Thomson, Renie, McFarlin and Devon.

Between 1882 and 1885 Robert L. Alexander R.S.A. lived at Greenbank Farm before moving to Canaan Grove. According to the *Dictionary of Scottish Art and Architecture,* by Peter McEwan, Alexander was born in Kilwinning in Ayrshire in 1840. He was apprenticed to a house painter, who also painted landscapes, but from 1868 he devoted himself to painting dogs and horses. He moved to Edinburgh where he began painting animals on commission and exhibiting at the Royal Scottish Academy. His greatest works are considered to be 'The Happy Mother' in 1887 and 'Two Mothers' in 1888, shortly after he left Greenbank. He died in Edinburgh in 1923 but was followed by his son, Edwin, who continued the tradition of painting birds and animals, among other subjects. He did not, however, inherit his father's longevity, as he died only three years after him at the age of 56. While Robert L. Alexander was at Greenbank, it seems possible that he was acquainted with another artist, Joseph Milne (1861–1911). Among Milne's many exhibited works was 'Early Spring in the Braidburn', possibly painted when he was at Nile Grove from 1902.

Greenbank also had a long line of tenant farmers, grieves and farm workers who lived in the numerous small cottages about the estate. The existence of the Moggie family is well documented. Daniel Moggie was born in 1868 at Cakemuir, Crichton, Midlothian and married Janet Adam of Tranent at Humbie on 8th October 1889. When they came to Greenbank Farm towards the end of the nineteenth century, Daniel worked, firstly, as a ploughman and then as the farm grieve. They had ten children (listed youngest first) – Daniel, Robina, Isabella, Matilda, Marion, John, Elizabeth, Janet, Agnes and Margaret – names which, from the back door, were shortened to Danny, Ruby or Beeny, Bell, Till, Mize, Jock, Liz, Jen, Ag and Mag. The children attended South Morningside School which was opened in 1892. Most of the family

Oxgangs Farmhouse and steadings, looking south from Oxgangs Road North, in September 1933. The farmhouse is now used as Oxgangs Police Station. Colinton Mains Drive had not yet been built.
Courtesy of Allison Naismith and Ian Mitchell, from the album of the late Joanna Wilson, formerly of No. 11 Greenbank Crescent.

On the right of the picture is No. 5 Greenbank Loan under construction by Robinson, the builder, and on the left is No. 52 Greenbank Crescent under construction by Keppie, the builder. Between the two is the roofless shell of Greenbank Farmhouse, c. 1934. *Courtesy of Elizabeth McIlwrick.*

attended St Matthew's Parish Church, now Cluny, in the days when the Rev. Duncan Campbell was capable of delivering fairly long sermons. Unable to afford the traditional Scottish antidote – the Pandrop – the Moggie children brought with them a wee poke of bacon rind, cut up into half-inch pieces, which they nibbled whenever the minister was about to emphasise what he had already emphasised. Bringing up ten children on a farm grieve's wage called for a certain degree of restraint in matters of finance. Mr Moggie's wage was 16/–d (80p) per week and the perks were a tied house and twelve bags of potatoes and twelve bags of turnips every year. Not only were the children encouraged to seek part-time employment when they were still at school, but after they had left the house and were making their way in life, they were expected to make a financial contribution to household expenses. If nothing else, it taught them ingenuity. When the girls of the family were getting to the stage where they wanted to experiment with make-up, they discovered that a reasonable result could be achieved by borrowing their mother's 'store book' and rubbing the red cover with a moist finger, sufficient to make the dye run; this was then applied as

Three farmers at Braid Farm, *c.* 1924. From left to right: Duncan Campbell of
Woodhall Farm, Juniper Green; William Wilkie of Braid Farm and Comiston
Farm; and Sandy Campbell of Corstorphine Bank Farm.
Courtesy of Miss Isla Wilkie.

Samuel Turner was born in 1859 in the Parish of Dundonald in Ayrshire. After spending some years in Africa, training young Africans in horticultural techniques, he came to Edinburgh where he ran a market garden at Plewlands. *Courtesy of James A. Bennet.*

a blusher. The 'store book', operated by St Cuthbert's Co-operative Association, had a more practical function: it allowed a week's credit for purchases to the value of the shares held. The limit was identified on the front of the book by one of a series of letters taken from the code word GLADSTONE: for example a £1 share had the letter G and a £5 share had the letter S.

There were lighter moments, of course, especially during the kirn-supper when each of the local farms took it in turn to hold the celebrations, after the harvest was safely in. When the Irish 'tattie howkers' were visiting, there were also frequent impromptu lessons for the children in the finer points of Irish dance and music. Perhaps the greatest occasion of all, however, was when the whole family got dressed up and walked all the way to Saughton to visit the Scottish National Exhibition during the summer of 1908.

Greenbank Farm and steadings from the air in the early 1930s. Several houses have been built on the east side of Greenbank Crescent but only two blocks on the west side, adjacent to the farmhouse. Part of the old City Poorhouse shows at the bottom of the picture. *Courtesy of the Edinburgh City Archivist.*

The artist, Robert L. Alexander R.S.A. (1840–1923), who specialised in painting animals, lived at Greenbank Farm between 1882 and 1885.
Courtesy of The Royal Scottish Academy.

When the family eventually left home, some of the girls went into nursing or service in and around the district of Morningside, but others left Edinburgh for pastures new. The Moggie family, perhaps more than any other, must have been acutely aware that their way of life, albeit hard, was under threat from urban development. They saw the building of the City Hospital, the opening of the Merchants of Edinburgh Golf Course, the construction of the Riselaw houses, and the slow, but certain, advance of houses, firstly up Greenbank Crescent from 1910, and later a plan to cover all the available farmland. Mr and Mrs Moggie and their yougest child, Daniel, left Greenbank Farm in 1926 and moved their worldly goods to a small flat in Miller Crescent. The last tenant farmer at Greenbank was Dick Boa whose family ran a wet dairy in Dorset Place. When he left the farm to go to West Linton in the early 1930s, the bungalows were nearly up to his front door.

The Moggie family's involvement at Greenbank was mirrored, at least in part, by the Carmichael family who lived at Hydropathic Cottages, now disused, at the west end of Glenlockhart Road. These

Janet and Daniel Moggie in 1933. They came to Greenbank Farm towards the end of the nineteenth century and there they brought up ten children. In 1926 they retired to Miller Crescent. *Courtesy of Lynne Common and Elizabeth Butchart, the great-granddaughters.*

Margaret Moggie, the eldest of ten children of Janet and Daniel Moggie, went to London where she had a successful career in nursing.
Courtesy of Bobby Moyes.

cottages, partly early nineteenth-century and partly much older, were also known as Slateford Cottages, a reminder that there had been no other houses between the Hydropathic and the old village of Slateford. The cottages are all that remain of Craiglockhart Farm, the farmhouse and steading having been demolished for the construction of the Hydropathic around 1880. Henry Carmichael was born in 1850 at Upper Grainston Farm, Kilbryde Estate, Dunblane, the second child of Daniel Carmichael and his wife Janet, née Bayne. He was married twice and fathered no fewer than fifteen children. His first marriage was to Catherine Gardner in 1871 who gave birth to thirteen children before dying prematurely in 1894 at the age of 43, from typhoid fever. In 1897 Henry married his second wife, Mary Comrie, from Blackford, Perthshire, who bore him a further two children.

Henry's rural upbringing dictated his work pattern during his entire working life. He started as a forester and then gardener at Dunblane Hydropathic where he was responsible for planting the avenue of trees from the roadside, for the owner James Bell. When James Bell bought Craiglockhart Hydropathic in 1891, Henry and his family moved to Craiglockhart where he was head gardener until his retirement in 1918. The youngest child of his first marriage was called Elizabeth Bell Carmichael as a tribute to James Bell, and an indication of the lifelong bond between Henry Carmichael and his employer. It is beyond doubt that Henry would have known the Hydropathic as a military hospital during the First World War when Siegfried Sassoon and Wilfred Owen were resident there under the care of Dr Rivers. The story has recently been retold in the very poignant film *Regeneration*. When Henry Carmichael retired to his boyhood home of Dunblane in 1918, his position

The Carmichael family of Craiglockhart photographed on the lower slope of Wester Craiglockhart Hill in 1892. Back row, left to right: Janet, Henry (father with Archibald on his knee), and Daniel. Middle row, left to right: Henry, William, Catherine (mother with Elizabeth on her knee), James and Robert. Front row, left to right: Margaret, Alexander, Catherine, Mary (Polly) and George. *Courtesy of Dr Peter Carmichael.*

On the left is Mary (Polly) Carmichael with her sister Margaret Carmichael, *c.* 1906, near Mid Lodge, Glenlockhart Road. In the background is the area of Easter Craiglockhart Hill, once known as Dove Croft, now part of the Merchants of Edinburgh Golf Course.
Courtesy of Dr Peter Carmichael.

was taken over by his sons, Robert and Alexander. They were later employed by the Convent of the Sacred Heart to prepare both the site and the grounds for the Convent. Robert continued as steward of the Training College until his retirement in 1941, completing fifty years' service by the Carmichael family. Henry died in 1925 and his second wife, Mary, in 1943.

Early in the twentieth century the western section of Greenbank Farm came under renewed pressure from house building. The first of the red sandstone houses on the east side of Greenbank Crescent were under construction in 1910 but building work was interrupted during the First World War (1914–1918). At that time most of the larger houses were built with accommodation for at least one servant, and such employment was commonplace. A few houses were built in the Crescent and nearby streets in the 1920s but it was not until the 1930s that the full building programme got under way. This was the era of the detached bungalow constructed by the builders Hepburn, Robinson, Irvine and Keppie. By the outbreak of the Second World War, in 1939, almost the entire district had been built up. One green oasis was Comiston Farm which still provided a rural setting from the south end of Greenbank Crescent almost to Swanston, without significant development. Housing at Comiston Farm was in two phases: firstly in the 1930s and later in the 1950s and early 1960s.

Greenbank and its environs can certainly be regarded as a settled area but it has not remained unaltered since it was built. Many of the first houses have been greatly extended and improved, and a few new houses have been built, usually on corner sites where the garden ground is larger than average. Two non-residential areas have changed, or are about to change, out of all recognition. The City Poorhouse in Glenlockhart Road has been transformed into The Steils and the City Hospital is scheduled for closure and redevelopment as residential accommodation.

Like any other part of the city, the development of Greenbank has taken place over a long period: the story of that development is described in more detail in the following chapters.

CHAPTER TWO

Braidburn Terrace to Braid Crescent; Greenbank Parish Church; Mortonhall Tennis Club; Hunter's Garage; Braid Hills Hotel; Riselaw

The 'eastern' section of the Lands of Greenbank lay between Braid Road and that part of Comiston Road now known as Greenbank Terrace and Pentland Terrace. Because it was separated from the larger part of the original Greenbank estate, it has developed differently. The street layout does not always follow exactly the boundaries of the old estates.

The first area to be developed was that between Braidburn Terrace and Braid Crescent, which included a variety of terraced houses by different builders and architects over a twenty-year period from about 1886. Next was the Braid Hills Hotel and the line of red sandstone terraced houses at the high-level section of Pentland Terrace. By 1900 the first Greenbank Church had been opened and a curling club was established in the low-lying ground to the south, where Mortonhall Tennis Club now is. By the beginning of the twentieth century more terraced houses were springing up in the streets of Riselaw followed by bungalows and villas in the 1920s and 1930s. The Braidburn Filling Station was opened in 1962 as an extension to the business of W. H. Hunter (Motors) Ltd., of Braid Road.

BRAIDBURN TERRACE TO BRAID CRESCENT

The streets between Braidburn Terrace and Braid Crescent were constructed by a variety of builders, most of them local to the area, between 1886 and 1906, on land which had previously formed part of the old estates of Greenbank, Plewlands and Braid.

Mr & Mrs McIlwrick and their daughter, Janet, and son, Hamish, outside their tenement flat at No. 9 Comiston Terrace in 1926. A few years later the McIlwrick family moved to Greenbank Crescent. *Courtesy of Elizabeth McIlwrick.*

Looking north down Comiston Road, *c.* 1904, with South Morningside Primary School on the left. On the right, the last section of Braid Crescent is still under construction, near the steps linking it with Comiston Road.
Courtesy of Alan Grant.

Much the same view a few years later, showing the corner shop, Aitkenhead the grocer, now occupied by Margiotta, the grocer. The left-hand lamp standard has a sign 'Cars Stop' which refers to the cable-car system, one of which appears in the earlier view. The last part of Braid Crescent was completed *c.* 1906.

Braidburn Terrace

Prior to 1905, the designation 'Braidburn Terrace' was applied to that section of the west side of Braid Road, immediately south of its junction with Braid Crescent. It also included the north-east section of present-day Braidburn Terrace. The remainder of the Terrace was known as Greenbank Road, taking its name from the narrow track which led to Greenbank Farm.

On the south side of the Terrace the first church was opened in 1900 and the larger church in 1927; both of them are discussed in detail later in the chapter. At the opposite end of the Terrace, a very grand house, Strathairly, was planned in 1903 for the artist, John Michael Brown of Strathairly, St Ronan's Terrace. He instructed his architect in February 1903 to draw up plans for the house, which were approved by the feuing architect, R. Rowand Anderson. Brown was an accomplished artist who exhibited frequently at the Royal Scottish Academy at The Mound. He was born in 1860 and studied at Glasgow College of Art where he met Jane Rae. The couple later married and then settled in Edinburgh. Many of Brown's pictures, particularly of golfing scenes, are now in great

The south side of Braidburn Terrace was designed in 1906 by W. H. A. Ross and built by David Adamson & Son of Morningside. At the extreme right-hand side of the photograph is the detached house, Strathairly, built in 1903 for the artist, John Michael Brown.

Braidburn Terra

demand. Interestingly, three of his pictures hang in a house not far from Strathairly. The pictures are: a water colour of Ballantrae; a water colour depicting the artist's niece and nephew on a beach in Ayrshire; and an oil under the title 'Glencraig'. Brown later left Strathairly and moved to No. 43 Pentland Terrace where he lived until about 1947. Strathairly was purchased by George Glen Napier who extended the library and other parts of the house in 1930. Napier was a man of considerable talent who had every need of an extended library. He was the author of several books, including *Homes and Haunts of Sir Walter Scott* and *Homes and Haunts of Tennyson*, and lectured widely on the poets Burns, Byron, Wordsworth, Tennyson and Scott. His interest in literature and heraldry increased greatly, later in life, after he had relinquished his interest in the family business of Napier & McIntyre, iron and steel merchants of Glasgow, founded by his father, James Smith Napier. George Glen Napier died in January 1941 at Strathairly, and was survived by his widow who resided there for many years thereafter.

The last part of Braidburn Terrace to be built was Nos. 2 to 20 on the south side. The builder was David Adamson & Son of Morningside and the architect was W. H. A. Ross of No. 21 Castle Street. The ten terraced houses were planned in 1906 with two storeys to the front and three to the rear. The natural fall in the ground level enabled the architect to include a basement floor to the rear with 'a larder, box-room, coals, washhouse, W.C., and servant's bedroom'.

Greenbank Place and Greenbank Terrace

Greenbank Place marks the boundary between the old estates of Plewlands and Greenbank. Because of the way in which the houses have been positioned in the surrounding streets, very few houses have an address in the Place. It was occupied from *c.*1887, No. 4 having an embellished date stone, 1886, above its front door.

Greenbank Terrace, forming part of Comiston Road, was built in two separate phases. The east side was constructed by James Slater, the builder, of No. 71 Albert Street, and houses were first occupied during 1886 and 1887. The west side of the Terrace was built much later as part of the development of Greenbank Crescent. The builder was William McNiven & Sons of No. 1 Yeaman Lane who obtained a feu charter from Colonel Trotter on 16th November 1906, to include a much bigger development extending into Greenbank Crescent and

Avenue. He obtained approval from the Dean of Guild to build the terraced houses Nos. 17 to 24 on 26th July 1906, but he never completed any other houses. Indeed, in 1914, there was an action against him in the Sheriff Court in Edinburgh of Declarator of Irritancy and Removing, as a result of which Mr McNiven lost his rights to build on the Crescent and the Avenue, on account of the long delay in completion.

Braidburn Crescent

The red sandstone terraced houses of Braidburn Crescent date from around 1887. One of the earliest feu charters, in 1886, was between the Trustees of the late John Gordon of Cluny and James Slater, the builder. Subsequent charters for the south-west corner of the Crescent involved William Stewart Cruikshank, whose company was responsible for the construction of the King's Theatre in 1906. The Crescent was built on land described as 'the Cottage Park of Braid in the Parish of St Cuthbert's', taking its name from Braid Cottage, which stood on the north corner of Braid Road and Braidburn Terrace. In 1890, the first owner of No. 8 Braidburn Crescent was Mistress Georgina Adams or Jolly, previously of No. 14 Upper Gilmore Place, widow of the Rev. James Jolly, formerly minister of Chalmers Memorial Free Church, which stood on the south side of the West Port.

In recent years, several papers and cards were found behind a fireplace in No. 4 Braidburn Crescent, which give an interesting insight into the Maclagan family who resided there from 1889. The general items include: a completed golf scorecard, by A. & D. Padon of St Andrew Square, Edinburgh, advertising the Allaway Patent Golf Ball for one shilling, 'Drives splendidly both down and against Wind'; several Wills's Cigarette cards including H. I. M. The Emperor of Russia; a Table of National War Bonds, 'What You Get Back' for the years 1918 to 1928; and a Christmas card, apparently to Bertie the dog, imploring him, in verse, to behave on Christmas Day! Items with a more local connection include: a ticket for a Social Meeting of St Matthew's Golf Club, to be held in the Church Hall on 14th November 1899; a voting card in favour of Sir Robert Finlay, parliamentary candidate for the Universities of Edinburgh and St Andrews; and a note to George Maclagan, dated 2nd January 1907, asking him to play in the 1st Cluny *v* Brunstane at Joppa on Saturday at 2.45 p.m., but the name of the sport is not mentioned.

The most interesting item, however, is a letter from Bob Maclagan, c/o Mr W. C. Sprinkle, Marshall, North Carolina, with a Lincoln five cents postage stamp, to his father John Maclagan, I. S. O. (Imperial Service Order) at No. 4 Braidburn Crescent. It highlights the potential conflict between a son's youthful ambitions abroad and a father's natural desire to share in the experience – whilst remaining in 'the old country'. The letter was penned on 9th February 1908 but could equally well have been 1808 or 2008. It is the epitome of Scottish male reserve, the inevitable legacy of a culture which has consistently discouraged the heart from evolving beyond its purely cardiac function:

My Dear Pater

What kind of weather are you having just now? We are having proper winter weather. It was very cold this morning and I think we will have more snow to day. Last Wednesday was a "corker" of a day ...

When the fact that I was teaching school here was announced in the papers, they gave me a very fine paragraph all to myself. They said that "Professor" Maclagan is a native of Scotland and a graduate of the Edin. University. They also paid me a number of compliments etc.

Bob did not enclose the newspaper cutting but continued his letter in much the same vein. The mask began to slip slightly but its fall was soon arrested:

You ask me what line my future work is going to take. Well, Pater, I hardly know myself. I have been thinking over it a great deal lately. I like farming very well, but I have not decided on anything yet.

I was sorry to hear about Ronnie Mearns. I hope he is better long before now.

I have not got your letter this week, but I expect it tomorrow or Tuesday.

Your loving son.

Bob

Braid Crescent, South Side

The south side of Braid Crescent, or High Level Terrace, as it was called at the planning stage, was built between 1887 and the turn of the century. Several builders were involved and many changes were made to the plans. First on the scene was John White, the builder, of No. 18 South Morningside Drive who instructed the architects George Beattie & Son to draw up plans for sixteen terraced houses, which were approved by the Dean of Guild on 24th February 1887. However, it would appear that only those houses up to, and including, No. 10 were completed at that time. The Crescent was continued westwards by another builder, John Scott of Maxwell Street, who applied to build further terraced villas in 1897 and 1900.

The west end of the Crescent was developed separately. The first idea, in 1891 by George Beattie & Son for Andrew Foster, was '5 continuous villas'. Beattie's drawings show three central villas, flanked at the east and west side by larger villas of two full storeys. The 1891 idea was never built. Beattie's second plan, for John White the builder, envisaged four terraced villas all of the same style, which were approved on 29th March 1894. In the end, only three were built (Nos. 36, 38 and 40) and the last feu (nearest to Greenbank Place) was filled by a detached house, No. 42. This house was designed in 1899 by P. R. McLaren of No. 34 St Andrew Square and probably built by John Scott for his own use.

Braid Crescent, North Side

The north side of Braid Crescent was begun at the east end in 1896, the corner feu being taken by David Adamson, the builder, of No. 42 Morningside Road. The line of the Crescent was continued westwards by John Scott in two phases, both designed by P. R. McLaren. The first phase, with the ornate overdoors, was approved in 1898, and the second phase, to the west, was approved in 1904.

No. 27, nearest to the flight of steps to Comiston Road, was first occupied by Dr Arthur J. Brock around 1906. Several years before that, John Y. Arnot, the builder, of No. 7 Belhaven Terrace, asked George Beattie to draw up plans for a very ornate development which was never implemented. The plans, dated February 1889, were approved by the Dean of Guild in May of the same year. The plan exploited to the full the vast difference in height between Braid Crescent and Comiston

Road. At the Comiston Road level a wide gateway was proposed, leading to a small courtyard and stable, above which was a loft and the coachman's room. The next storey was a conservatory at the level of Braid Crescent which communicated with the main house, to be built on two storeys with attic dormers. Had the full scheme been implemented, the stable entrance could have become a major problem for modern-day traffic at that point on Comiston Road.

GREENBANK PARISH CHURCH

Greenbank Parish Church, on the south corner of Braidburn Terrace and Comiston Road, dates from 1927: the origin of the church, however, can be traced to the last few years of the nineteenth century. It owes its existence to two members, in particular, of Braid United Presbyterian Church – William Forrest and Joseph Bennet – who were keen to see a new congregation established in the growing suburbs to the south of Morningside Station. There was some opposition to the choice of site, which was considered, by some, to be too far south, even allowing for the anticipated increase in population. At its September meeting in 1898, however, the Presbytery decided to go ahead and 'to take steps to open a station with a view to the erection of a congregation'. The plan was relatively modest. To begin with, a hall was to be built which would be used for worship until the time was right to build a more permanent, larger church. The architect's drawings, dated November and December 1898, bear the address No. 24 George Street but, unfortunately, do not disclose the name of the firm. Descendants of the Bennet family have always understood that the design was the work of Joseph Bennet's son, John Bennet. The Dean of Guild approved the plans on 19th January 1899 'to erect on the corner area of ground, situated on the south side of Greenbank Road and on the east side of Comiston Road, Edinburgh, a stone and brick built and slated Church Hall and Offices, adjacent to and in connection with the new United Presbyterian Church to be erected hereafter on said area'. The completed building was entered from Greenbank Road, now Braidburn Terrace. At ground level the plans show a central corridor flanked, on the left, by the session room, and on the right by the vestry. Subsequently, the use of these two rooms was altered so that the room on the right was the session room and that on the left was the board room. Beyond was the main

John H. Bennet who succeeded his father, Joseph Bennet, as Managing Director of Messrs Alder & Mackay, Gas Meter Manufacturers, of Gorgie. Joseph Bennet was an early benefactor of Greenbank Church whose family installed a stained-glass window in the south aisle in his memory. *Courtesy of Mrs M. E. Elgin.*

hall with a gallery at the north end, and the pulpit was placed centrally at the south end. In the basement area there was a smaller hall, a kitchen and a heating chamber. The total cost was £3,595 reduced by the sum of £1,200, gifted by Mr Bennet. The feu charter, dated 16th December 1899, from the trustees of the deceased John Gordon of Cluny, contained the usual mixture of rights and responsibilities: John Bennet was given 'the right to quarry stone or sand for the purpose of building thereon and not otherwise'; but he was also obliged 'to keep the [perimeter] railings open to let the grass or flower plots be seen from the Carriage roads'.

The new church, or station, was opened on Sunday 13th May 1900 under the charge of David S. Brown, 'a student on the verge of licence', at a salary of £100 per annum. In July of the same year the congregation achieved full status as Greenbank United Presbyterian Church. Within a very short time, however, in October 1900, it was renamed Greenbank United Free Church at the historic union of the United Presbyterian Church and the Free Church. Greenbank's first minister, the Rev. Norman Fraser from Saffronhall United Free Church in Airdrie, was inducted on 20th February 1902 and held office until 1913 when he was transferred to Mount Pleasant Presbyterian Church, Liverpool. In 1913 the congregation numbered 300.

Greenbank's second minister was the Rev. Thomas Ratcliffe Barnett who came from St Andrew's United Free Church in Bo'ness on 21st January 1914 and remained until his retirement in 1938. It was a long and eventful ministry, taking in the years of the First World War, and later, the building of the new church. Shortly after Mr Barnett's arrival at Greenbank, in the summer of 1916, he was appointed a Chaplain to H. M. Forces and did not return to Edinburgh until the autumn of 1919. During the war years, no progress was made on the intended new church building. However, early in 1920 a decision was taken to explore the possibility of enlarging the existing Hall by the addition of two transepts. The idea was to alter the orientation of the church to an east/west axis by building an extension to the west. The centre of the existing Hall was to become the nave, and the north and south ends were to become the new transepts. It was a novel idea which was costed at £6,500 or £2,000 more than was in the building fund. Despite the scheme being approved in principle, it was decided at a Special Congregational Meeting on 6th November 1923 to build a completely new church, to

seat about 600, leaving the Hall accommodation unaltered. As the
building fund was still only slightly more than half of the estimated
costs of £12,000, it was decided to delay implementation until at least
75% of the costs were subscribed. That meant that £2,500 was still
needed. By the time the architect, A. Lorne Campbell, had drawn up
definite plans and agreed contracts with Gerard, the builder, the costs
had risen to £14,000, which still left £3,500 to be raised by the congregation. The biggest fund-raising event was the Grand Bazaar held in
Braid Church Hall on 31st October and 1st November 1924 which set
a target of £1,000 but raised almost twice as much. More modest events
had equal commitment: in one sketch the children were dressed as

Laying the
foundation stone of
Greenbank United
Free Church on 24th
April 1926 by the
Rev. James Harvey
D. D., Moderator of
the United Free
Church. The church
was designed by
A. Lorne Campbell
and built by Wm.
Gerard & Sons.
*Photograph by
George Blyth Logie.
Courtesy of
Greenbank Parish
Church.*

different coins and had to somersault into a collecting box, but the tiny farthing somersaulted off the platform into the audience. The foundation stone was laid in the west gable on 24th April 1926 by the Rev. James Harvey D.D., Moderator of the United Free Church. As work progressed, the entire cost of the building had not yet been subscribed, but help was on hand. Timing the announcement to perfection, a member of the congregation handed in a blank cheque with a request that an announcement should be made that the church was then free of debt. The church was dedicated on Saturday 8th October 1927 by the Rev. James Weatherhead D.D., Moderator of the General Assembly. The congregation's sense of achievement was, however, almost dashed when Dr Barnett received an urgent message, early on the morning of 14th January 1929, that the church was on fire. By the time he covered the short distance to Braidburn Terrace the fire tenders were already there. Fortunately, the outbreak was confined to the gallery area of the old Hall and little or no damage had been caused to the new church.

Dr Barnett spent a great deal of his time building up the various organisations within the church. In 1927 the congregation totalled 500, rising to 850 by the time he retired on 31st December 1938. In addition to his work in the parish, Dr Barnett was an accomplished author with more than a dozen titles to his name, including *Margaret of Scotland, Queen and Saint*, in 1926 and *The Story of the Covenant*, in 1928.

In 1939, shortly after the retirement of Dr Barnett, Greenbank elected a new minister, the Rev. David H. C. Read of Coldstream West, who remained for the next decade. Mr Read was born in 1910 in Cupar, Fife but was educated at Daniel Stewart's College, Edinburgh and Edinburgh University, after which he attended Summer Seminars in Montpelier, Paris, Strasbourg and Marburg. He discovered, like his predecessor Dr Barnett, that his early days at Greenbank were overtaken by events outwith his control – this time the outbreak of the Second World War. As a Territorial Army Chaplain he was called up almost immediately, which delayed his induction until 5th October 1939. Thereafter, he was abroad, where he was held in a prisoner-of-war camp and did not return to Edinburgh until 1945. In his absence, services were taken, firstly by Dr Barnett, and then, after he became ill, by the Rev. Dr George S. Stewart and the Rev. Dr William Orr. When Mr Read returned to Greenbank, one of his first projects was to form a

The huge timber beams of the nave are slowly being surrounded by the supporting masonry of Greenbank United Free Church. On the right is the foundation stone and the builder's board 'Wm. Gerard & Sons, Main Contractor', of Wheatfield Street. *Courtesy of Greenbank Parish Church.*

Greenbank Parish Church, in its modern setting, on the south corner of Braidburn Terrace and Pentland Terrace. *Courtesy of Greenbank Parish Church.*

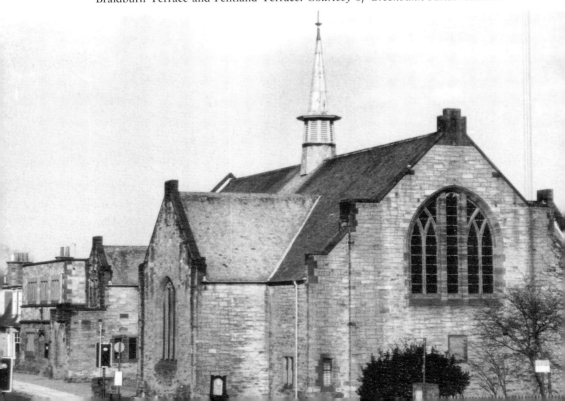

'Minister's Bible Class' for young members of the congregation. They later adopted the name *Quest* which was taken from a series of talks given by Mr Read in 1942 at an Officers' Prisoner-of-War Camp near Kassel, in Germany. In later years Mr Read was widely acknowledged as a talented broadcaster and speaker. He left Greenbank in September 1949 to become the first Chaplain of Edinburgh University. He later became minister of the prestigious Madison Avenue Presbyterian Church in New York and a well-known writer and broadcaster in the United States.

The vacancy was filled by the Rev. Donald G. M. Mackay, whose ministry at Greenbank spanned thirty-two years until his retirement in 1982. During that time Greenbank underwent considerable expansion, both in the number of members, and the facilities available. Mr Mackay was a son of the manse, whose father was the Rev. Dr William Mackintosh Mackay of Sherbrooke Church, Glasgow. Prior to coming to Greenbank he was at Carden Place Church in Aberdeen. When writing

Some of the enthusiastic volunteers, outside the church halls, who helped to collect the huge consignment of clothing for Hungary at the time of the uprising in 1956. *Courtesy of Greenbank Parish Church.*

in *The Story of Greenbank* in 1990 Mr Mackay recalled, when he first
came to Greenbank, how different it was from the small 'settled' congregation which he had left in Aberdeen. At Greenbank the
congregation was over 1,000 and increasing rapidly in size and influence.
Bearing in mind the advice given to young missionaries: 'For the first
two years keep your ears open and your mouth shut', he endeavoured
'to abide by this in spirit if not in letter'. He relates details of three
important events all occurring in the first year of office: 8th January
1950, the unveiling and dedication of a Memorial to Dr Ratcliffe Barnett
in the form of a bronze bas-relief portrait by James A. Clark A.R.S.A.;
12th November 1950, the dedication of the congregation's War Memorial, comprising two stained-glass windows in the vestibule; and lastly,
the Congregational Jubilee celebrations on 18th and 19th October. It
was also a time when the Fabric Committee was seldom idle. A complete redecoration of the church interior was undertaken in 1953 by
William H. Kininmonth (later Sir), and in 1958 the Upper Hall was
opened at a cost of £5,000. In the 1970s, another hall to the south of
the church was opened, and the original organ was refurbished and
modernised. Mr Mackay faithfully records all these happenings in the
second part of *The Story of Greenbank* which he devotes to his own
ministry. He recalls all the events and the people who made them all
possible in a series of informative and amusing anecdotes. Perhaps his
most unguarded moment was during the last farewell organised by the
congregation for his retiral on 30th June 1982. Entering the church for
a final evening social, he was confronted by a jumbo-size 'pulpit fall'
with the startling legend, GRAND RETIRAL SALE – EVERYTHING MUST
GO – and go he did – but not until the end of the party.

In 1988 Mr Mackay wrote a *Guide to the Stained Glass Windows in
Greenbank Parish Church, Edinburgh* giving details of the benefactors
and the artists involved. There are six windows in all: South Aisle –
The Ministry of Music Window, 1928 by James Ballantyne Jnr., in
memory of Mr & Mrs Joseph Bennet, by their daughters, Mrs Har-
greaves and Mrs McKechney; South Transept – *The Pilgrim's Progress
Window*, 1934, by Alexander Strachan, gifted by Mrs Clark in memory
of her husband Dr W. Inglis Clark; Chancel – *The Revelation Window*,
1928, by Alexander Strachan, gifted by Dr & Mrs W. Inglis Clark in
memory of their only son Capt. Charles Inglis Clark; North Transept –
The Parables Window, 1954, by William Wilson, gifted by Mrs

The present minister, the Rev. Ian G. Scott, B.Sc., B.D., S.T.M., photographed at the time of his induction to Greenbank Parish Church in January 1983.

T. D. Dobson in memory of her husband Thomas Douglas Dobson; North Aisle – *The Nativity Window,* 1957, by William Wilson, given to the congregation in a bequest by Mr John Lyon of Greenbank Lane; and Vestibule – *The War Memorial Window,* 1950, by William Wilson, to the men of Greenbank who fell in both World Wars.

Greenbank's present minister, the Rev. Ian Gray Scott, was inducted on 26th January 1983, having previously been minister at Holburn Central Parish Church in Aberdeen. Ian Scott was born on 31st May 1941 in Kirkcaldy, Fife where he was educated at the High School before going to St Andrews University. At university he graduated B.Sc. in Mathematics and Astronomy but, not content with a life of 'counting and keeking', he entered the Faculty of Divinity at St Mary's College where he graduated B.D. with distinction in 1964. Later he attended Union Theological Seminary, New York, graduating S.T.M. (Master of Sacred Theology) in 1965.

After serving for a year as Assistant to the Rev. Peter Brodie at St Mungo's Parish Church, Alloa, Mr Scott was inducted to his first charge, Holy Trinity Parish Church, Bridge of Allan in June 1966. In 1976 he became minister of Holburn Central Parish Church until he came to Greenbank. Ian Scott married Sandra Angus in Aberdeen in 1979 and their daughter, Alison, was born in February 1983, a month after they came to Edinburgh. In addition to his parish work, Ian Scott has held a number of other church appointments, including: Convener of the Panel on Doctrine of the General Assembly, from 1978 to 1982; Vice-Convener of the Committee on Education for the Ministry from 1989 to 1992; Vice-Convener of the Board of Education from 1988 to 1991; Convener of the Board of Parish Education from 1993 to 1997; and Member of the Joint Commission on Doctrine.

Under Mr Scott, Greenbank Parish Church maintains a high level of involvement in the community, due, in no small way, to its ability to hold its existing membership of over 1,000, and to attract new younger members. Departing from trends found elsewhere, the Sunday School, now renamed *Spectrum,* has a growing attendance, divided into three departments by school year rather than strict age. The former Bible Class, renamed *Springboard,* takes young adults from the first three years of secondary education. There is a natural progression to *Q11,* a youth group founded in succession to *Quest* and *Junior Quest,* established many years ago by the Rev. David Read. *Q11* has a long tradition of involvement with matters of social concern, for example homelessness, Milestone House and work camps in Budapest in 1995, and South Carolina in 1997, as well as in rural parts of Scotland. In September 1995, present members of *Q11* met with former members of *Quest* to celebrate the 50th anniversary of the founding of *Quest*, with a celebratory dinner at Napier University, and a Thanksgiving Service at Greenbank on Sunday 24th September. The Rev. David Read attended, and spoke at both events.

The various halls at Greenbank are also in constant demand for local organisations. The Greenbank Playgroup for pre-school children was started by the congregation in the early 1970s and continues to this day, while the Nursery Department of South Morningside School has been accommodated in one of the halls since 1997. The Neighbourhood Group was started in 1971 by Mrs Fay Paterson to provide transport for elderly or infirm people needing to keep hospital appointments etc. It is staffed by volunteer drivers and helpers from Greenbank and other churches in the Morningside area. The 'Homeless Group' was established in 1993 to find ways of caring for the homeless through existing agencies. Later, the A.B.C. Group was formed (A Break for Carers) to provide a group of 'sitters' to enable those caring for ill or elderly relatives or friends to have an occasional break. An information leaflet is published giving full details of all church activities and organisations. Of particular concern to Greenbank Church and others was the closure, after thirty-two years, of the City Hospital Tearoom which was started by Greenbank, with later assistance from the churches of Colinton Mains, Juniper Green and Craiglockhart. Over the years more than £100,000 was donated to the hospital from the profits made by the Tearoom, staffed by almost 250 volunteers.

MORTONHALL TENNIS CLUB AND CURLING POND COTTAGE

Mortonhall Tennis Club is situated beside the Braid Burn on a low-lying triangular piece of ground to the south of Greenbank Parish Church. Whilst the 'Braidburn Triangle' is hardly on a par with the Bermuda Triangle, nevertheless it has not yet revealed all its mysteries. The ground forms part of the natural valley of the Braid Burn which was artificially stopped up, at its south-west end, by the construction of

Pentland Terrace in the nineteenth century. The narrow, north-east end
of the ground (near the junction of Braid Road and Braidburn Terrace)
was occupied for many years by a small dairy which was owned by the
Duff family, among others. A more substantial, stone and slated house
stood at the Pentland Terrace end. Early maps refer to it as the Curling
House but its general appearance suggests that it may have pre-dated
the curling pond era. The *Edinburgh and Leith Post Office Directory
Map* of 1896 shows the outline of the curling pond, and the same
directories list Robert Ferguson, Mason, Slater & Chimney Sweep (business address No. 164 Morningside Road) living at Curling Pond Cottage
between *c.*1890 and *c.*1920. Thereafter, Curling Pond Cottage (or House
as it was sometimes called) was renamed Braidburn Cottage, during the
occupancy of Mrs R. Robertson, who ran a confectioner's business from
No. 140 Comiston Road.

No records of the Curling Club have been traced but it seems likely
that it existed sometime between 1890 and around 1914. Margaret
Warrender, who wrote *Walks near Edinburgh* in 1895, states: 'On the
opposite side of the road [Braid Road] is the pond belonging to Morton
Hall Curling Club', but, unfortunately, she does not provide any more
information. Exactly when the rinks were drained and the first tennis
court was laid remains a mystery. Although Mortonhall Tennis Club's
records suggest that the club was formed in 1926, there is cogent evidence to suggest that tennis was being played there from at least 1913
or 1914. Firstly, there is a well-documented photograph, known to date
from 1913, showing a tennis group at the Mortonhall site. Secondly, in
the club records there is a 1949 reference to an application under Section
55 of the Town & Country Planning (Scotland) Act of 1947. In answer
to a question on capital expenditure, the club states: 'Laying of Tennis
Courts 1914' and 'Extension of Pavilion 1930'. The same documentation
confirms that Curling Pond Cottage was leased at a rent of £12 per
annum, with forty days' notice on either side.

Although the Minute Books of Mortonhall Tennis Club have been
missing for some years, the original feu charter for the ground is known
to have been registered on 21st May 1926. In it, the Trustees of the late
John Gordon of Cluny grant the piece of land to the Trustees of
Mortonhall Lawn Tennis Club for the purpose of playing lawn tennis.
The feuars were bound to maintain the buildings on the feu and were
'not permitted any cowshed, pighouse, shed or house for masons,

Morton Hall Curling Club Pond lay to the south of the first Greenbank United Presbyterian Church. The south side of Braidburn Terrace has not yet been built, suggesting that the photograph was taken between 1900 and 1906. *Courtesy of Greenbank Parish Church.*

Anyone for tennis? An elegantly dressed group at the site of Mortonhall Tennis Club in 1913. *Courtesy of Miss Margaret Bell.*

wrights, coopers, weavers or any slaughterhouse, crackling house, making glue, cudbear [another name for *orchil*, a purplish dye] or bricks'. For many years the ground floor of Braidburn Cottage was used as the club rooms and the upper storey was leased to a tenant.

The modern history of the club dates from the mid-1950s when a decision was taken to demolish Braidburn Cottage and replace it with a more suitable clubhouse. Plans were drawn up by the architect, A. N. Willoughby, in September 1957, and permission to demolish Braidburn Cottage was approved by the Dean of Guild on 4th October 1957, enabling the new clubhouse to be built in the same position. The entrance path and stairs from Comiston Road were moved slightly to the north. The accommodation included a committee room, a common room, male and female changing rooms and showers, and a verandah overlooking the courts. The new clubhouse was opened by Mrs Pringle, wife of Craigie Pringle, then President of the East of Scotland Lawn Tennis Association. Subsequently, the committee room and common room were opened out into one larger room.

In 1977 the club's five courts were changed from the very labour-intensive blaes surface to an all-weather surface. The improvement was instrumental in the setting up of the Mortonhall Junior Open Tournament which was hosted by the club from 1978 to 1992. The courts were again resurfaced in 1994–95 and floodlighting was installed on the two courts nearest to the clubhouse in 1996. In 1993 a wall was constructed on the north bank of the Braid Burn to protect the courts from the flooding which has occurred on several occasions over the years.

At the present day there are about 200 members and the club competes in various tournaments. These include: Ladies', Men's, Girls' and Boys' teams in the East of Scotland Lawn Tennis Asociation Leagues; a ladies' team in the Veteran League; and teams in the Social Mixed and Winter Leagues. Numerous tournaments are also held within the club membership. The club badge depicts the heron whose habitat includes the Hermitage and Mortonhall area.

W. H. HUNTER (MOTORS) LTD

Before the Gulf Service Station in Pentland Terrace was opened in 1990 the site was occupied by the Braidburn Service Station, owned by the Hunter family who can trace their association with the motor trade

James Hunter, at the front, and his co-rider, Willie Smith, at Loanhead on the *Hunter Special* built by James Hunter. He won the Waverley Roads Club gold medal in 1897 for covering 100 miles in 5 hours and 25 minutes. *Courtesy of Bill Hunter.*

back to its infancy at the beginning of the twentieth century. The firm was established in 1919 by William Hay Hunter whose family were pioneers in the early days of mechanical transport. William's father was James Hunter, a blacksmith to trade, who specialised in building bicycles and tandems; and his grandfather, William Hunter, ran horse-drawn buses from Waverley Bridge to various small towns on the outskirts of Edinburgh. William Hay Hunter, born in 1891, served his apprenticeship with Robert Wight Jnr., Automobile Engineers in East Newington Place, before enlisting with the Army Service Corps at the beginning of the First World War. After war service he started up in business on his own, operating from two modest huts in a pend off Balcarres Street between 1919 and 1921. The opening entries from Hunter's first invoice book suggest that the mechanised transport of the day still had some distance to go!

Mr J.Beveridge, 8 Cluny Drive, Edinburgh

1919 June 4
To time in going to Gullane and inspecting car .. £1: 1: − [£1.05p]

Hire of motor cycle for journey .... 10/− [50p]

1919 June 5
To time in going to Gullane for car................. 15/− [75p]
Train and tram fares .... 2/6d [12½p]

After considering, but declining, the chance of a more spacious site on the corner of Balcarres Street and Morningside Road (later occupied by Baird the Bootmaker, followed by the Bank of Scotland), Mr Hunter had a new garage built, designed by P. R. McLaren of No. 34 St Andrew Square, on the south corner of Braid Road and Comiston Terrace. This was opened in 1922 at a time when the surrounding area had already been built up as tenements. Before the garage was built, the site was occupied by the remnants of 'the tin kirk', built in 1896 by Messrs Speirs & Co., Iron Building Contractors, No. 125 West Regent Street, Glasgow, as an offshoot of Christ Church at Holy Corner.

Bill Hunter joined his father in the business in 1946 when the trade was still recovering from the constraints of the war years. Although the garage remained open during the Second World War, very few people were entitled to buy fuel, and the normal work of car maintenance was replaced by Government contracts to make unidentified parts for the war effort. As petrol was strictly rationed, the pumps were mainly used to supply the fire and ambulance services and the local doctors. Even in the post-war era, the public's perception of the motor car was very different to that of the present day. Ownership of a car was considered to be for recreational purposes rather than an essential of life, and its use was very much orientated towards the summer months. It was common practice to 'lay up' vehicles from October to March each year with consequent savings in the running costs. At the beginning of each winter Bill Hunter would visit his customers and prepare the car, by draining the radiator, disconnecting the battery, pumping up the tyres

William Hay Hunter, founder of the firm W. H. Hunter (Motors) Ltd., inspecting a 1908 Stanley 10-h.p. Gentleman's Speedy Roadster at the Braid Road premises *c.* 1950. The steam-driven car is still in the possession of the Hunter family. *Courtesy of Bill Hunter.*

and putting the vehicle up on blocks in the garage, where it remained until the spring. In these days cars were not fitted with heated rear windows, or heaters, and the windscreen wipers and 'semaphore' indicators often froze completely.

By the 1950s it was clear that further expansion of the business was desirable to keep pace with the increase in car ownership. A field to the south of Mortonhall Tennis Club was bought in 1950 with a view to building a new two-storey garage with access from Braid Road and Pentland Terrace, but planning permission was not granted. The Braidburn Service station with four pumps was opened in 1962 and continued until the present Gulf Service Station was built in 1990.

In 1997 the main garage in Braid Road was closed, and clearance of the site began for the construction of flatted dwellings, bringing to an end nearly eighty years of continuous service by three generations of the Hunter family, Bill Hunter's son Alistair having joined the firm in 1984. Fortunately, many associations and momentoes remain. The work

The premises of W. H. Hunter (Motors) Ltd. were operated, on the south corner of Braid Road and Comiston Terrace, by three generations of the Hunter family between 1922 and 1997. The premises were demolished in 1998. The photograph, taken in the mid-1980s, shows several Morgan sports cars outside the garage and under the canopy. *Courtesy of Bill Hunter.*

benches which originally came from East Fortune Aerodrome were returned there for the use of the Museum of Flight. One particularly interesting item has remained in the family since 1936, namely a 1908 Stanley 10-h.p. Gentleman's Speedy Roadster made by the Stanley Steam Car Company. The car, which belonged originally to Lord Antrim, is believed to be the only complete, roadworthy, steam-driven car in Scotland.

BRAID HILLS HOTEL

According to the Edinburgh volume of *The Buildings of Scotland*, the Braid Hills Hotel was designed by W. Hamilton Beattie in 1886. There is, however, doubt as to when it was actually built and opened. It appears for the first time on the *Edinburgh & Leith Post Office*

Directory Map of 1894, and early descriptions of the hotel suggest that it was opened in 1897. It is beyond doubt, however, that one of its early attractions was the proximity of the golf courses on the Braid Hills. Appropriately, the hotel has two stained-glass windows depicting golf scenes which include the professional, James Braid, who first won the Open in 1901 at Muirfield. When the Braid Hills Hotel was first opened it stood alone, in a very commanding position, surrounded by the fields of Braid Farm and Greenbank Farm. There were no housing developments between the hotel and the present city boundary. As early as 1898 the proprietors embarked on the first programme of extensions which have been a feature of its development over the years. The alterations, designed by the architect George A. Lyle, involved 'the removal of the roof from part of the present buildings and the addition of two floors consisting of bedrooms and sitting rooms with bathroom and lavatory accommodation'. A washing house and cycle house was also built.

Not long after the hotel was opened, a *Descriptive Brochure Concerning the Braid Hills Hotel as a Health Resort* was written by Jessie Patrick Findlay and published by Young & Irving of Edinburgh. Its preamble makes interesting reading:

The South side of Edinburgh has long been noted for its salubrious

The Braid Hills Hotel was designed by W. Hamilton Beattie in 1886 in a very prominent position with commanding views over the city. The glasshouse was removed when a new dining room was built in 1986.

climate. In bygone days when the city boasted the pomp and circumstance of a Scottish Court, the old Scots Lords were wont to send their delicate wives and daughters 'furth o' the Borough Muir' to regain health and strength. The locality still retains the character of being a favoured and peculiarly health-giving retreat, not only for the benefit of the delicate, as of old, but also for the robust who may desire to spend their superfluous energies in such hardy pursuits as golfing, cycling and walking, for which this district is so eminently suitable. It was with a view to meeting the growing demands of pleasure-seekers and visitors in search of the picturesque that the Braid Hills Hotel has recently been erected.

The *Tariff* included: Breakfast from 1/6d to 2/6d; Lunch, Hot or Cold, from 1/6d to 3/– ; Afternoon Tea 1/– ; and Dinner from 2/6d to 4/–. The *Terms* were: Per day 10/– ; Sat. to Mon. 18/– ; Fri. to Mon. £1:6:-d; Board, per week from £2:12:6d; Sitting Rooms, per day, 4/– to 7/6d; and Servant's Board, per day, 5/–. Visitors had the use of a spacious coffee room, drawing room, billiard room, reading room and smoking room, furnished throughout by John Taylor & Son of Princes Street.

The special attractions included drives into the country. The local tour was fairly modest: round the Braid Hills, via Liberton and the Grange at 4/– (20p) per hour for a one-horse single fare, and 5/– (25p) per hour for a pair of horses. Other destinations, at the same rates, included Habbie's Howe, the Forth Bridge, the Post Office and Swanston, but for the more adventurous, all-day excursions, with an emphasis on the east coast, could be arranged: Cockenzie, 30/–; Aberlady, 35/–; Gullane, 40/–; and Dirleton, 50/–. The hotel incorporated a six-stall stable, coach-house and hay loft, with a separate two-roomed dwelling for the coachman.

Unfortunately, the brochure is not dated but it mentions that 'cable tramways are about to be built', which suggests that it was written shortly after the 1898 hotel extensions. The cable car extension from Morningside Station to the Braid Hills Hotel was authorised in 1897 and was under trial in 1899. The author of the brochure also refers to the hotel architect as George A. Lyle, whereas he appears to have been the architect of the 1898 extension. Later brochures state that the cable car service ran every three minutes up to 11.30 p.m.

Further alterations were made to the hotel in 1923 to convert the

billiard room, laundry and servants' hall into a new dining room and
to rearrange other parts of the hotel. Over the years an annexe has been
developed by acquiring the northernmost houses in the high-level
section of Pentland Terrace. At one time eight terraced houses formed
part of the hotel but this has now been restricted to six, with a com-
municating section built in 1982. A new dining room to seat seventy,
built in 1986 on the west elevation, was designed by the architect, John
Tod, and built by B. M. Construction in a style sympathetic to the
original design.

   The hotel has always been in private hands and has attracted many
visitors of international fame. Muriel Spark was a frequent visitor and
Rachmaninov is said to have left a lasting impression when two windows had to be removed to allow his grand piano to be put into his
room. It is said that for one *breve* moment his heart missed a beat as
his entourage fought to stave off disaster!

RISELAW

The houses of Riselaw, between Braid Road and Comiston Road, were
constructed between 1897 and 1937 in a variety of styles by different
architects, and often constructed by local builders. The terraced houses
were built first, followed by the villas and the bungalows.

Pentland Terrace

The road known as Pentland Terrace was constructed in 1830, but it
was a long time after that before any houses were built. They began in
1897 beside the Braid Hills Hotel, and continued southwards to the
junction with Riselaw Crescent around 1923. The architects' plans show
the position of the estate wall along the line of the east pavement.

   The high-level section of Pentland Terrace was planned in 1897, not
long after the construction of the hotel. The seven northernmost terraced
houses were designed by the architect, D. M. Sutherland, and constructed by the Dunfermline builders, William Birrell and James Smith.
The most southerly section was designed about the same time by George
A. Lyle, incorporating a date stone, 1897, on the south gable. In 1910,
a most unusual application was made to the Dean of Guild by Miss
Joanna Wilson 'to erect a temporary iron and wood building' in the
garden ground of her house, No. 1 Pentland Terrace. The prefabricated

An early example of the service 16 electric tram at the Braids terminus in Pentland Terrace. On the upper deck of the open-topped trams there were waterproof aprons, attached to the back of the seat in front, which could be drawn out to protect the knees of the passengers from rain and snow. Also in the picture is a service 13 tram, this service having been extended to the Braids from Tollcross on 18th March 1923, before becoming the Granton/Churchhill circle early in 1924. *Photograph by the late E. O. Catford. Courtesy of Alan Brotchie.*

structure was supplied by Speirs & Co., of Glasgow, Structural Engineers, Designers and Erectors of Composite Iron and Wood Buildings. It communicated with No. 1 and included a hallway, a large living room-cum-kitchen with a fireplace, a bathroom and a store. What its function was, adjacent to a house which already had accommodation on three floors, has not been established.

The remaining, lower section of Pentland Terrace was built in three phases, separated by each of the side streets. The terraced houses, between Braid Hills Road and Riselaw Road, were designed by Lyle & Constable in 1903 and built by W. G. Davies of No. 13 Craiglea Drive. The next section, with the red-tiled pitched roofs, between the Road and the Place, were designed in 1909 by P. R. McLaren and built by John C. White of No. 23 Comiston Drive. The final section, between the Place and the Crescent, was much later: the three north-most blocks were by Wainwright & Williamson, Civil Engineers, of No. 65 Frederick Street in 1923; and the three south-most blocks were designed in 1923 by John A. W. Grant and built by The Scottish Garden City Housing Society Ltd., of No. 28 Castle Street.

Braid Hills Road

The north side of Braid Hills Road began with No. 1 as part of the 1897 Pentland Terrace development. Nos. 13 and 15 were built along with the terraced houses, to the north, in Braid Road. They were all designed by W. B. Campbell of Pit Cairn, Colinton, in 1907, and constructed by The West End Building Co. Ltd., of Edinburgh. The same architect and builder continued the line of terraced houses, northwards, in Braid Road. The south side of Braid Hills Road was developed along with Nos. 168, 170 and 172 Braid Road. The date was 1905, the architect was Lyle & Constable, and the builder, W. G. Davies of Craiglea Drive.

Riselaw Road

The north side of Riselaw Road was also designed by Lyle & Constable and built by W. G. Davies. No terraced houses were built on the south side, the available ground being taken up by Nos. 176–198 (even) Braid Road, designed by P. R. McLaren in 1912 and built by John C. White. Only one bungalow was built on the south side, designed in 1927 by the architect Thomas Graham, for the petitioner George Rae of No. 45 Castle Street.

Riselaw Place and Terrace

The south end of Riselaw was built much later and reflects the changes in architecture and the growing popularity of the bungalow style of house, many of which have spectacular views of the city from their elevated positions. This is particularly true of the houses on the east side of Riselaw Place, planned from north to south between 1926 and 1930.

Riselaw Terrace was designed by several architects and built in the same era, most of the building warrants being granted between 1928 and 1930. The west side was built mainly by William White Hamilton, the joiner, of No. 30 Polwarth Gardens, who also constructed two houses on the east side, near the island shrubbery. The remainder of the east side was built by two developers, Alexander Sim of No. 47 Pentland Terrace and George Martin of No. 12 Saughtonhall Grove.

Riselaw Crescent

Riselaw Crescent has several styles of architecture planned between

The fields of Greenbank Farm and Comiston Farm from the high-level section of Pentland Terrace, probably in the 1920s before the main bungalow development began. Comiston Farmhouse can be seen in the top-left corner of the picture in front of the belt of trees.
Photograph by Iain Hosack. Courtesy of Flora MacCormick.

Car No. 41 was built at Shrubhill, in Edinburgh, and first entered service in 1935. It is seen here on service No. 15 at the Braids terminus *en route* for King's Road, Portobello. On the right is the passenger shelter and the tram stop sign which reads 'CARS TO TOWN STOP HERE'. *Photograph by R. J. S. Wiseman.*

1923 and 1937. The greatest number of houses were semi-detached, two-storey villas, designed by James K. Stewart of No. 34 Spottiswoode Street in 1923 and 1924, and built by Alexander Sim. These included the blocks on the north side and probably Nos. 14 and 16 on the south side. Also on the south side were Nos. 6–12, developed by James Alexander Morton in 1923 and 1924. Detached houses were built at the top end (nearest to Braid Road) in 1925 and 1926, and, later, at the bottom end (nearest to Comiston Road) around 1937. A very distinctive house, No. 12A, in the Bauhaus style, by the architect, W. Norman Hunter of Meadowfield Avenue, was constructed in 1954 on a piece of ground which had been a quarry and was completely overgrown by whin bushes. Originally, planning permission had been given to construct two dwelling houses. In 1936 plans for one house only were

Two fashionable ladies alight from service No. 16 from town at the Braid Hills Hotel stop. This tram was built by Hurst Nelson of Motherwell and first entered service in 1936. The sign on the standard says 'CARS STOP BY REQUEST'. The photograph was taken on Whitsunday 24th May 1953 at a time when private cars were much less numerous than today. *Photograph by R. J. S. Wiseman.*

approved but were never implemented. The drawings, by the architect Walter W. Reid of Frederick Street, envisaged a house of six main apartments (with maid's room) on various levels to suit the contours of the site. The roofline was to have a frieze of vertical red brick, and be capped by a 'pagoda' style tower.

CHAPTER THREE

The Streets of Greenbank

The Scottish Record Office holds an early plan of Greenbank entitled *Plan of Greenbank Proposed to be Feued 1886,* drawn by the architect Robert R. Raeburn of Charlotte Square. It is divided into 13 plots and covers an area of just over 148 acres, including an old road along the line of present-day Braidburn Terrace, Greenbank Crescent and Greenbank Loan. This old road led from Braid Road to Greenbank farmhouse and steadings. Although the plan was authorised in 1887, it was not until 1908 that any real progress was made to implement the scheme. Prior to that, the entire area between Pentland Terrace, in the east, and the City Hospital, in the west, was arable farmland, supporting a small population of farm workers, all of whom were eventually decanted as building work progressed.

Early in 1908 the land superior, Major (later Colonel) Algernon Richard Trotter of Mortonhall, arranged for his solicitors to draw up feu charters to regulate the manner in which the area was to be developed. Very strict conditions were imposed regarding the position and design of the houses, their value and insurance arrangements, the selection of materials, and the payment of feu duties. The builders were also required to provide access paths for the use of the householders prior to completion of the permanent roads and pavements. Most of the early houses were built by small local firms whereas the later phases attracted much bigger developers. A strict building timetable was also imposed by Colonel Trotter who was still responsible to the tenant farmer 'for compensation at his outgoing in respect of loss of crop, unexhausted manure etc.'. In practice, the time limits were often relaxed where the delay was not caused by the fault of the builder. There were also frequent changes in the road layout, notably around the area of Greenbank Avenue, and at the south end of Greenbank Crescent where Greenbank View was to be constructed as a cul-de-sac nearly opposite the mouth of Greenbank Road, in a style similar to Greenbank Rise. Greenbank View, which would have had about six or seven houses, was never built. Before any construction work could commence, the builder was required to submit, to the Dean of Guild, architects'

The thatched Greenbank Cottage stood in what is now the back garden ground
of Nos 17 & 19 Greenbank Crescent until *c.* 1910 when it was demolished to
make way for the construction of Greenbank Crescent. One half of the cottage
was the home of the local midwife.

drawings giving details of the site plan, the elevations and a description
of the intended accommodation. Approval was frequently subject to
alteration in design and methods of construction.

Greenbank Terrace and Place were described in Chapter 2. The
remainder of Greenbank was built in two phases: the first phase included parts of Greenbank Crescent and Avenue between 1908 and
1929; and the second phase progressed southwards in the 1930s.

THE FIRST PHASE, 1908—1929

The first part of Greenbank to be built began on the east side of the
Crescent, which was formed along the line of the access road to Greenbank Farm. The houses were substantial two-storey semi-detached
villas, built of natural stone and roofed with slate, with an insurance
value of £950 each. The first four blocks (Nos. 1–15) were designed by
W. H. A. Ross of Castle Street, approved by the Dean of Guild in 1908,

Robert White (1873–1953), the founding principal of Robert White & Co. S.S.C., of No. 32 Queen Street, Edinburgh, lived at No. 31 Greenbank Crescent for many years. He is seen here visiting the home of his friend Thomas McIlwrick of No. 50 Greenbank Crescent. *Courtesy of Elizabeth McIlwrick and Mrs Marjory Daly.*

and built by David Adamson of Morningside Road. Nos. 17–23 were also scheduled to be completed by the same architect and builder, but there was a slight delay because the proposed feu already contained two old houses. One was the thatched Greenbank Cottage and the other, to the west, was a slightly larger range of cottages with a slated roof. In the meantime, however, in 1909, David Burton, the builder from Meadowbank Avenue, continued with four blocks (Nos. 25–39) designed by James Moscrip & Sons of Hanover Street. Moscrip's site plan shows a new road (which was never built) off the west side of the Crescent.

Neither Adamson, nor Burton, appears to have built any other houses in either the first or second phases, but the east line of the Crescent was continued by the builder John Gavine of Morningside Road. His first development was Nos. 41–51 designed by the architect P. R. McLaren of St Andrew Square, whose 1912 drawings included a servant's room off the kitchen area. Mr Gavine had hoped to complete another four similar blocks on the west side of the Crescent but his plans, dated 1914, were cut short by the outbreak of the First World War. He completed two blocks (Nos. 56–62), first numbered as 44–50, but it was soon evident that he was not going to have sufficient men or materials to finish the job. In some desperation he asked his solicitor to contact Colonel Trotter on 11th May 1916:

> In view of the very exceptional circumstances consequent upon the War and since the Feu Charter was granted, our client has found it quite impossible to continue to build, the cost of material and scarcity of labour being such that building operations could only be carried on at great loss, besides being discouraged by the Government.

Fortunately, Colonel Trotter agreed to release Mr Gavine from the terms of the feu charter. In a subsequent letter, dated 24th May 1919, Mr Gavine was invited to 'restate his interest in continuing' but he does not appear to have done so.

At the end of the First World War the Greenbank feuing plan was slow to recover. In the 1920s it was confined mainly to Greenbank Avenue, parts of the Drive, and the west side of the Crescent. Two blocks (Nos. 4–10) in the Crescent were built during 1923 and 1924 by John Russell Turner from Morningside Road, following designs by the architect William Anderson of Falcon Gardens. That was followed by Wainwright & Williamson's development at Nos. 12–18, the Crescent, which also included Nos. 1–8, the Avenue. These were flatted dwellings, each block containing four houses to a capital value not less than £700 for each house. Mr Wainwright was a civil engineer and Mr Williamson was an architect, both operating from No. 65 Frederick Street. A few years later, in 1928, Wainwright & Williamson returned to complete similar blocks at Nos. 1–12, the Drive, and thereafter Nos. 13–24.

In the 1920s, only one house, a bungalow at No. 53, was built on the east side of the Crescent, on a very commanding site near the brow of the hill. The feu charter, stipulating that the capital value of the house was to be not less than £1,500, was signed on 22nd December 1925 in favour of Mrs Mary Helm Scott or Wright, wife of James

Wright of No. 104 Comiston Road. Unfortunately, the identity of the builder was not disclosed. The architect, however, was Hunter-Crawford & Williamson of Frederick Street whose plans, in October 1925, showed a 'maid's bedroom' to the rear of the house and a 'maid's sitting room' to the front. Before approving the plans for this very elegant house, the Dean of Guild stipulated that the 'Maid's W.C. should be placed inside the dwelling house'. The Register of Sasines, dated 7th April 1931, confirms that at this point in the Crescent Colonel Trotter's new proposal was to extend Greenbank Crescent at a width of 40 feet only and not 60 feet as originally proposed.

THE BUILDERS IN THE SECOND PHASE

The builders and the architects involved in the first phase of Greenbank have already been mentioned. However, during the second phase (1930–1940) over 400 houses were completed, including various styles of detached bungalows, semi-detached bungalows, semi-detached villas and flatted villas. By far the greatest number were detached bungalows. The four main builders in the second phase were Hepburn Brothers Ltd., Richard Robinson and his son Richard J. Robinson, Theodore K. Irvine and Simon Keppie & Son.

Hepburn Brothers Ltd

The Hepburn story begins with Alexander Innes Hepburn, a farm grieve, and his wife Margaret (née Low) from Dollar, both of whom later moved to Dunfermline. They had seven children: Catherine, born 1883; Lawrence, born 1885; James, born 1887; Jean, born 1889; Alexander, born 1893; Margaret, born 1895; and John, born 1897. In the 1920s, the two eldest sons, Lawrence and James, set up the Hepdon Concrete Company in Dunfermline to manufacture pre-cast lintels and sills for the construction industry. They later went into house building, and in 1931 Hepburn Brothers Ltd. was established with all four brothers as directors. Lawrence was Managing Director, James was Works Director, Alexander was Sales Director, and John was Company Secretary. Their first address was Pittencrieff Street, Dunfermline, then No. 94 Chalmers Street, Dunfermline until 1932 when a serious fire destroyed the premises. Thereafter, the workshop was at Westfield Road in Edinburgh, and the office was at No. 95 Shandwick Place, then No. 56 George Street and

Bowlers, cigars, waistcoats and walking sticks are all part of the uniform of this group of young men photographed at Dunfermline in the early part of the nineteenth century. The gentleman on the left is James Hepburn, and the gentleman in the centre (front) is Lawrence Hepburn, both of Hepburn Bros., the builders. The identity of the others is not known. *Courtesy of Alex Hepburn.*

later No. 32 Alva Street. During the 1930s Hepburn built extensively throughout Edinburgh, at Craigentinny, Kingsknowe, Blackhall, Corstorphine, Craiglockhart and Greenbank. At the height of the building programme they were completing houses at the rate of one every day. Over 500 tradesmen were employed covering all the basic trades. Rates of pay for skilled tradesmen were £3: 6: 8d (£3.33p) per week, and for labourers £2: 10/– (£2.50p) per week in 1933. In 1939, at the outbreak of the Second World War, domestic house building was stopped and did not restart until 1945. By then materials were very scarce and there were Government restrictions on the type of building allowed. John Hepburn died in 1945 and in the following year James's son, Alex, and Alexander's son, Sandy, joined the firm as directors. As most of Hepburn's land bank had been used up, they diversified into Public Works until 1965 when the firm went into voluntary liquidation.

At Greenbank, Hepburn built all the houses in the Grove, Park, Rise and Row, and part of the Crescent, Gardens and Road. The draughtsman responsible for the house designs was Thomas Bruce of Inverkeithing. The Hepburn brothers all lived in houses constructed by the firm, but not at Greenbank.

Richard Robinson and Richard J. Robinson

The Robinson family moved from their native Yorkshire in the mid-1800s to work a farm, The Moy, Tamnamore at Dungannon in County Tyrone. There were three daughters, Rachel, Ruth and Matilda, and two sons, Richard and Tom. As the farm could not support two additional families, Tom emigrated to Canada where he established a canning factory. The elder son, Richard, came to Edinburgh in the 1890s, becoming a time-served journeyman stonemason and builder. He worked on two of Edinburgh's most prestigious building contracts of the day: firstly, the City Hospital at Greenbank, designed by the City Architect, Robert Morham, and built between 1896 and 1903; and later at the Usher Hall, designed by J. Stockdale Harrison, and built between 1910 and 1914. With the experience gained he decided, around 1916, to set up in business on his own, confining himself, initially, to small contracts for the repair and renovation of private houses. He progressed to building 'Arthurstane' at Braid Hills Avenue and four semi-detached houses at Buckstone Terrace, opposite the present East of Scotland Water Authority.

When Richard Robinson first came to Edinburgh he lived at Bellfield Lane, in Portobello, but later married and set up home at No. 2 Millar Place. There were four sons of the family, William, Richard, George and John, the second eldest (Richard John Robinson) joining his father in the business. They built at Kingsknowe, Camus, Longstone, Fairmile Avenue, Paties Road, Buckstone Terrace, and two large semi-detached houses at the corner of Buckstone Drive and Braid Road. Their offices were at No. 5 Alva Street and the yard was in Jordan Lane. The foreman joiner, Sandy Richardson, worked with the Robinsons for many years.

At Greenbank the Robinsons built at the Drive, Lane, Loan and Road in the 1930s. At that time, Richard Snr. lived at Paties Road and later Longstone and Winchburgh where he died in 1946 aged seventy. Richard Jnr. lived at No. 10 Greenbank Loan which had a specially built billiard room to the front of the house. Thereafter, he lived at Abbotsford Crescent before emigrating to Australia in 1948. Descendants of the family still reside in and around Greenbank.

Richard J. Robinson worked with his father, also Richard, in the construction of bungalows at Greenbank in the 1930s. He is photographed here in 1927 when he was best man at the wedding of his brother, William. *Courtesy of the Robinson Family.*

William Robinson, eldest son of Richard Robinson the builder (and brother of Richard J. Robinson), on the day of his wedding to Agnes Angus on 16th September 1927. *Courtesy of the Robinson Family.*

Theodore K. Irvine

When Theodore K. Irvine, a native of Lerwick, came to Edinburgh as a young man, he qualified as an architect and set up his own business as a builder and architect. He moved to Bathgate where he maintained his business interests and also taught building construction at evening classes. Later he was one of the founding members of the Scottish Society of Bathgate, and Worthy Master of Torphichen Kilwinning Lodge of Freemasons. He joined Bathgate Town Council in 1922 where he served as convenor of several committees before being elected as Provost of Bathgate in 1937. During a lifelong association with the town he designed several public buildings, including the Emporium Buildings at the corner of Whitburn Road and George Place, and the Evangelical Union Congregational Manse. He was appointed clerk of works for the construction of Petershill Reservoir No. 2 and Ballencrieff Reservoir.

Theodore K. Irvine, a native of Lerwick, came to Edinburgh where he qualified
as an architect and set up in business as a builder and architect. He later moved
to Bathgate where he held the position of Provost from 1937 until his death in
1939. He built houses in Greenbank Crescent and Greenbank Road. *Courtesy of
West Lothian Council Libraries.*

The house at No. 103 Queensferry Road, built by Theodore K. Irvine, was intended for his own use, but he died in 1939 before occupying it. *Courtesy of Mrs A. H. Rushbrook.*

Provost Irvine also maintained a strong connection with Edinburgh where he kept an office at No. 2 Robertson Avenue for the administration of his building programme at Duddingston and Greenbank. At Greenbank in the 1930s he designed and built Nos. 20–30 (even), the Crescent, and in the Road, Nos. 21–33 (odd) and Nos. 8–26 (even) but excluding No. 20 which was built by Ford & Torrie of Queen Street for the Napier family. Irvine's nephew acted as the clerk of works, but Irvine inspected all the houses personally. In the feu charter signed by Theodore K. Irvine in 1932 there is one of the few references to a Government scheme, presumably introduced to stimulate house building in the 1930s, 'value of houses to be £750 i.e. £650 purchase, plus £100 Government Grant'.

Unfortunately, Provost Irvine did not see out his term of office at Bathgate as he took seriously ill in his Robertson Avenue office one afternoon and died on 28th June 1939 at the age of 56. At the date of his death he was still very much at the centre of his career in the building industry and had begun the construction of a very grand baronial-style house in Queensferry Road, intended for his own use, but which he never occupied.

Three generations – all Simon Keppie – at Yewlands Gardens, Liberton, c. 1930. The two men were father and son in the building firm of Simon Keppie & Son. The third Simon Keppie was a pupil at the Royal High School when the photograph was taken: later in life he qualified as an actuary and became an Assistant General Manager with the Standard Life Assurance Company of Edinburgh. *Courtesy of J. C. Keppie.*

Simon Keppie & Son

Simon Keppie Snr. was born on 8th February 1852, a son of Peter Keppie, plumber and gasfitter, of Nicolson Street, Edinburgh. Simon started in business as a house carpenter at No. 4 Gibbs Entry and progressed from there to have his own business from around 1880. He was a cousin of John Keppie, R.S.A., the Glasgow architect (1863–1945), and his artist sister, Jessie Keppie (1868–1951).

Simon Keppie Snr. and his wife Alice, née Cockburn, had two daughters and four sons, Simon Jnr. following into his father's business around 1900. As Simon Keppie & Son at No. 65 St Leonard's Street they built extensively in various parts of Edinburgh, notably at Willowbrae, Liberton, Wakefield Avenue and Greenbank. Simon Snr. lived at Yewlands Gardens in Liberton but one of his sons, John Keppie, lived at No. 2 Greenbank Loan, built by the firm in 1933. John was also the owner of the newsagent's shop in Comiston Road, under the name Lennox, but later Alexander's. At Greenbank in the 1930s, Simon Keppie built Nos. 2–8 (even), the Loan, and Nos. 32–54 (even), the Crescent, part of which was the site abandoned by John Gavine, the builder, at the outbreak of the First World War. Simon Keppie Jnr. lived latterly at No. 86 Liberton Brae, and when he died in 1948 the firm was absorbed into George Bee & Co., also of St Leonard's Street.

THE SECOND PHASE, 1930–1939

It was during the decade immediately prior to the Second World War that the district of Greenbank was laid out in its present form. During this period the remaining fields of Greenbank Farm were gradually taken out of production and the old farmhouse and steadings demolished. Between 1930 and 1935 all the feu charters were signed between Colonel Trotter and the prospective developers. For the most part, they were established builders who had already completed houses in various parts of Edinburgh. In addition, there were a few sites, notably in Greenbank Crescent, which appear to have been developed directly by the first owners. Contrary to popular belief, the main developers did not build speculatively, but, rather, in response to specific demand. This caused a number of problems: prospective buyers frequently asked for minor variations to be made whilst their houses were in the course of erection; some asked for their house to be positioned differently, especially if it was on a corner site; and some even asked for the same style of house to be built in a different street. At least one family decided to opt for a different feu when they discovered that the height of the roof of the house opposite was going to spoil their view of the Pentland Hills.

The feu charters specified the time in which the houses were to be completed. Although the time was quite short (less than one year), it did not usually present a problem to a builder who had negotiated only a few plots. However, for the bigger builders the time limits became more difficult to attain when the demand for houses unexpectedly slackened. The trouble began to show in 1935 during the construction of parts of Greenbank Row and Grove. When Hepburn, the builder, began to have difficulty in selling his more expensive houses, he contacted Colonel Trotter with a view to varying the terms of the feu charter to allow the construction of fewer of the more expensive types. After agreeing the concession, Colonel Trotter's solicitor continued:

> As these concessions are very considerable we trust that your clients [Hepburn] will now be able to proceed with the completion of the schemes. Our client [Colonel Trotter] mentions that he considers the arrears of building in Greenbank Crescent and Greenbank Gardens are very serious. The position in the Crescent is that twenty-seven houses should have been erected by Martinmas 1934 and only one has in fact been erected. In Greenbank Gardens all the houses should have been completed by Martinmas 1934 and eight have not yet been commenced. Colonel Trotter instructs us to say that unless there is a marked progress in these building areas by Whitsunday next he may require to take steps in the matter.

Hepburn Bros. built all their houses to a very high specification but, naturally, there were houses of different values, to attract the widest possible interest from the public. What Hepburn had not bargained for was that one of their clients might take exception to the practice of varying the master plan after it had been announced. The inevitable clash came in 1937 when M bought one of Hepburn's six-apartment houses only to discover that next door to him was to be a house of only four apartments, instead of the intended six. M contacted the Dean of Guild Court and submitted details of his case, alleging 'it is a four apartment house, whereas M's is a six apartment house, and its erection will seriously prejudice the amenity and depreciate the value of M's property'. M pointed out that he and his wife had been attracted by the site at Greenbank but were 'apprehensive lest it should be spoiled by the erection of houses of an inferior type'. The Court considered the case at some length but decided in favour of Hepburn on the basis that M had no title to object to any variation in the feu charter agreed between Hepburn and Colonel Trotter. The Court held that: 'In order to entitle a neighbouring proprietor to object he must shew that the original contract by which the restrictions were imposed was intended for his benefit and to confer a *jus quaesitum* [a special law] on him'. In the circumstances of the case, the Court decided that it did not.

Greenbank Crescent: East Side

The east side of Greenbank Crescent was completed up to and including No. 53 during the first phase. One of the first houses to be completed in the second phase was No. 55 for Miss Margaret White of Rochester Terrace, whose architect, Henry & MacLennan, drew up the plans in June 1928. The next group of houses, Nos. 57–69, were all developed

Margaret Finlay, with young Frances Baillie, on the pavement outside the Baillie family home at No. 113 Greenbank Crescent in 1938. In the background, the Crescent stops short of the Braid Burn, beyond which are the fields of Comiston Farm. *Courtesy of Mrs Frances Gould, née Baillie.*

by William Patterson, the architect, of Observatory Road, on a piece
of ground to the north of Fly Walk (opposite Greenbank Park). Patterson also designed bungalows in Observatory Road and villas on the
south side of Frogston Road.

South of Fly Walk, the Crescent was completed by Hepburn, the
builder, the feu charter dated 12th December 1933 dictating the standard
of housing required: 'the said dwelling houses shall be varied in design
and outline and of an artistic and pleasing style of architecture and ...
the east elevations shall in particular be varied and attractive'. Natural
stone was to be used and the capital value of each house was to be
between £1,200 and £1,300. The absence of No. 85 is accounted for by
the fact that the feu charter allowed for one semi-detached block to be
built, whereas Hepburn received orders for detached houses only on
this section. In the Minute of Waiver, Colonel Trotter's signature is
witnessed by Stanley Ager, 'my butler', and Harriet Agnes Frost, 'my
housekeeper'. Although the feu charter was signed in 1933, the last of
the houses was not completed until 1939. The final section (Nos. 101–
117) was feued in 1934 and 1935 to include a short cul-de-sac,
Greenbank View, which was never built. The plans envisaged about six
houses, partly on ground now occupied as Braidburn Valley Park.

Greenbank Crescent: West Side
During the first phase, the west side of the Crescent was developed
sporadically, and it was not until the second phase that an overall plan
was implemented. It began in 1931 with Simon Keppie building six
blocks of semi-detached villas, Nos. 32–54, designed by A. Murray
Hardie of 20 George Street. That was followed by Theodore K. Irvine's
development (Nos. 20–30) in the mid-1930s which included houses in
Greenbank Road. Also in the mid-1930s were Nos. 64–82, forming part
of William Patterson's development on the east side. Houses south of
Greenbank Park were all built by Hepburn Bros. The feu charter was
signed in 1933 but some of the houses were not completed until six or
seven years later. On 5th November 1938 Hepburn contacted Colonel
Trotter to report on the delay in completing the houses and secured a
dispensation for No. 106 which 'shall be erected and completed not
later than the term of Candlemas 1940'. Colonel Trotter, who was still
a substantial landowner in the 1930s, took the chance to point out that
he had other sites available: 'in view of the concessions I have made to

Messrs Hepburn Bros., I hope they will inform their clients that there are good building sites to be had in the neighbourhood of Fairmilehead'.

Greenbank Road

Greenbank Road was completed during the second phase, mainly by three builders, Theodore K. Irvine, Richard J. Robinson and Hepburn Bros. Each builder developed both sides of the road together, in sections, starting at the north end. Most of the feu charters were signed between 1932 and 1934, although the entire street was not finished until about 1939. The greatest number of people moved into their new homes in 1933 and 1934. There were many changes to the plan and several small sites were developed out of chronological sequence. For the most part, the houses (four, five and six-apartment bungalows) were designed by the builders' own draughtsmen rather than by firms of architects. The exceptions were Nos. 36–46 and Nos. 49–59 which were designed by George M. Wilson of Queen Street for Robinson, the builder.

For reasons which are not now obvious, Nos. 2–6 (even) and Nos. 1–19 (odd) were never allocated. The north end of the Road, Nos. 8–26

Nos. 11 & 13 Greenbank Row have just been completed by Hepburn Bros., and the front gardens have been laid out. The remainder of the north side of the Row (to the east) has not yet been built. Photographed from the driveway of No. 9 in 1934. *Courtesy of Robert Watson.*

The rear view of Nos. 6 & 8 Greenbank Gardens built by Hepburn Bros., in 1932. No. 8, on the right, is finished externally but No. 6 has still to be slated and harled. *Courtesy of W. Hoffie.*

Maggie Neil visiting the Tullis family home, 'Thorwick', in 1933, at No. 67 Greenbank Road, built by Robinson the builder. Note that the road and pavement have not yet been made up.
Courtesy of Miss Margaret Tullis.

Margaret Tullis and her aunt, also Margaret Tullis, in the fields of Greenbank Farm at the back of No. 55 Greenbank Road, *c.* 1933. *Courtesy of Miss Margaret Tullis.*

(excluding No. 20) and Nos. 21–33, was built by Theodore K. Irvine as part of a bigger development extending into Greenbank Crescent. Operating in the Road at about the same time was Richard J. Robinson who built Nos. 28–66 and Nos. 35–79. Feu charters for all these houses were signed in 1932 and 1933 and the Dean of Guild approved the plans shortly thereafter. No. 20 was built by Ford & Torrie in 1933. The dividing line between houses by Robinson and those by Hepburn was the small lane which joins Greenbank Road to that part of the Drive leading to the City Hospital. South of this lane was Hepburn territory, forming part of his most ambitious building programme which included the Park, Grove, Row and Rise.

Greenbank Drive and Lane

Most of the flatted dwellings, Nos. 1–24 Greenbank Drive, were completed during the first phase. In the second phase plans for ten bungalows (Nos. 25–34) were given approval by the Dean of Guild at the end of 1929, and Richard Robinson began construction almost immediately. The relevant documents describe the street as City Hospital Road. Following on from Richard Robinson was his son, Richard J. Robinson, who applied to the Dean of Guild to complete the line of the Drive with a further eleven houses. These were designed in September 1930 by the architect, G. Murray Wilson, of No. 2 Charlotte Square. Almost simultaneously, Richard J. Robinson gained approval for eleven similar bungalows in the Lane, most of which were occupied between 1932 and 1934.

Greenbank Loan and Gardens

Greenbank Loan was built by Richard J. Robinson and Simon Keppie & Son. Keppie built the block of four flatted villas (Nos. 2–8) from

A family photograph taken in the back garden of No. 53 Greenbank Road: Mrs Jane Macdonald with three daughters, younger son, and four grandchildren. Back row, left to right: Jean Macdonald, Janet and Tom Macdonald, Jean Kerr, Margaret Harkness, Robert (Bob) Harkness. Front row, left to right: Mrs Rubina Harkness, Mrs Jane Macdonald, Morag Macdonald, Mrs Jemima Kerr. *Courtesy of Dr Morag M. Macdonald.*

Janet McIlwrick of Greenbank Crescent arrives, with her father Thomas McIlwrick, at St Matthew's Parish Church (now Cluny) on her wedding day in 1941. *Courtesy of Elizabeth McIlwrick.*

In the 1930s motor cars were not common but they were substantial. This
Wolseley 18/80 saloon car, registration number BSC 798, in the driveway of No.
50 Greenbank Crescent, cost £295, plus tax, in 1936.
Courtesy of Eric McIlwrick.

1933 to designs by A. Murray Hardie. Also in 1933 Richard J. Robinson
obtained a feu charter for the remainder of the Loan in which he built
36 houses. The plans were first approved in February 1933 but there
were several substitutions, including a revised plan for No. 10 for Mr
Robinson's own occupation. The plans, dated September 1933, by
Richard J. Robinson, contained a specially designed billiard room with
a fireplace recess and an en suite toilet. The floor of the billiard
room was specially strengthened by a series of brick piers from the
foundations to the underside of the floor timbers.

Greenbank Gardens was built by Hepburn Bros. with a few houses
(Nos. 40–44) by Richard J. Robinson as part of his development in the
Loan. The feu charters were signed by Hepburn as early as June 1933
but work was slow to be completed, partly because of lack of demand.
The final result, however, is a very attractive range of houses, particularly where the roadway is widened out at the 'dog leg' bend. The
houses were priced from £650 to £950 when first built.

During the construction of part of the Loan and the Gardens, Greenbank farmhouse and steadings were still standing, though not in use. Permission to demolish the steadings was granted on 6th January 1933, and for the farmhouse on 18th May 1934. The farm buildings and courtyard stood on ground now occupied by the houses and gardens of Nos. 11 and 13 the Loan, and Nos. 40–44 the Gardens.

Greenbank Park, Grove, Row and Rise

All the houses in the Park, Grove, Row and Rise were built by Hepburn Bros. in conjunction with their developments in the Crescent and Road. Large numbers of houses were planned, in blocks, without the need to do drawings for each individual house. Hepburn advertised several styles of house, usually of four or five apartments, and these were included in the master plan and sales brochures. However, there were many alterations and substitutions before the houses were completed in 1939. Out of a block of 99 houses approved by the Dean of Guild in 1932, about 20 had been altered in some way before completion. After the first feu charter was signed in 1932, progress was made southwards to include the Grove, the Row and the Rise. The plan was implemented according to demand and most streets remained incomplete for some time. The first of the owners moved in during 1932 and 1933 but some were as late as 1939.

THE SALES BROCHURES

It is unlikely that the smaller builders issued anything like a modern sales brochure for their houses: it is more likely that prospective purchasers were invited to inspect a similar house at the nearest location. Hepburn Brothers, however, took great pride in their sales literature and issued several brochures, a few of which have survived. There was a comprehensive booklet, with a brightly coloured cover, running to more than fifty pages with details of the districts in which houses were being built, diagrams and plans of the various houses, a description of the accommodation, the prices, and a list of the fixtures and fittings supplied as standard. There was also a series of advertisements of the day to tempt buyers to furnish their new homes with the very latest in household gadgetry. Throughout the brochure Hepburn extols the virtues of owning the last word in house construction:

The front cover of the sales brochure issued by Hepburn Bros. in the 1930s advertising their bungalows in various parts of Edinburgh, including Greenbank. Prices ranged from £560 to £950. *Courtesy of John L. Marlow.*

The largest of our residences are all specifically designed and arranged to replace the depressing Victorian house with its damp, dark cellars, long corridors, and windowless staircase.

Hepburn also liked to point out that there was money, time and effort to be saved:

Gas and electricity in the modern house is equivalent to the saving of a maid, or alternatively, the saving of drudgery to the housewife.

And if all else failed there was an appeal to good old-fashioned common sense:

Monotony of diet is bad for the health – monotony of surroundings is bad for the nerves.

In 1932 prices were advertised between £560 and £950. The cheapest house, at £560, was a semi-detached three-roomed bungalow with kitchen and bathroom, or £585 if detached. At the top end of the market was Hepburn's '6-apartment cottage' with a very desirable specification: four clothes poles in the garden; ground fenced all round; double gates to own driveway; four rooms with open fires; two rooms with electric

A Site with a Magnificent View . . . and Convenient, too!

GREENBANK, MORNINGSIDE, forms an Ideal Housing Site. Situated on the South Side of Edinburgh, with a lovely Open View of the Pentland Hills, it is bordered by the Braids and Craiglockhart Hill. The Site is far enough from the City to enjoy a country and peaceful aspect, while at the same time being most convenient for Tram and 'Bus Services to all points. We would welcome the opportunity of conveying you to View this gloriously healthy site. May we? Please phone hour most convenient.

Hepburn's sales brochure included this photograph, taken from Pentland Terrace, of houses in the course of erection on the east side of Greenbank Crescent. *Courtesy of Alex Hepburn.*

Part of the same scene in 1998 photographed from Riselaw Road. *Photograph by Phyllis M. Cant.*

fires; lamps and plain shades to each pendant; blind rollers on every window; 'Ready-to-Work' kitchenette and larder; china cabinets in drawing room; and all walls papered at 2/– (10p) a roll.

There were also numerous advertisements offering 10% discount

Lunn's offered a 10% discount – provided you were flitting to a Hepburn bungalow. Reproduced from the sales brochure. *Courtesy of Stanley Clark.*

The Hepburn sales brochure included a large selection of advertisements for furniture and electrical appliances. J. & R. Allan of South Bridge could provide a complete bedroom suite for £38.55p. *Courtesy of Mrs Jessie Campbell.*

The above room was furnished by J. & R. Allan, Ltd., in one of our Exhibition Houses.

The living room of a Hepburn show-house in Greenbank Grove in the early 1930s as displayed in the sales brochure. *Courtesy of Miss Catherine Glen and Mr and Mrs Johnstone.*

More than sixty years on – in a similar house – are the sisters Joanna and Kathryn O'Brien, 1998. *Photograph by Phyllis M. Cant.*

from Lunn's Removals for anyone going to a Hepburn house; green-houses for £12:15/– (£12.75p); and Corkoleum 'to deaden the sound of footsteps' at 10½d (4p) per square yard. A separate leaflet, dated 1934, from the Dunfermline Building Society offered 90% loans over a period of 25 years. For Hepburn's most expensive house, at £950, the deposit was £95 and the four-weekly repayments were £4: 13: 6d (£4.67p).

OUT WITH THE OLD: IN WITH THE NEW

There was a further price to pay and that was the complete destruction of Greenbank Farm and a way of life which had been in existence for many generations. In fairness, however, it must be remembered that the eventual demise of the farm was evident as early as the early part of the nineteenth century, when schemes were being considered for a 'New Road to Penicuik'. The idea was to construct a more direct route (now Comiston Road and Pentland Terrace) from Morningside Station to Buckstone and Fairmilehead, avoiding the steep inclines and awkward bends of the old Braid Road. The construction of Pentland Terrace completely dissected the fields of Greenbank Farm, alienating the east section (Riselaw) from the main farm. The construction of Greenbank Crescent from 1908 removed two of the most picturesque farm dwellings overlooking the Braid Burn. The tenants were probably rehoused in the new double cottage built in 1909 to the west of the steadings. The new cottages each had two rooms, heated by open coal fires, a small scullery, a coal cellar, an ashpit and an 'earth closet apartment'. By 1933 bungalows were being built right up to the edge of the farmhouse and steadings. Colonel Trotter obtained permission from the Dean of Guild to demolish the farm steadings in January 1933, but a decision on the old farmhouse was delayed in the hope that it could be renovated to form part of the new district of Greenbank. Unfortunately, nothing came of the idea and permission to demolish was granted on 18th May 1934. A steam roller, with special spikes on its rear wheels, was used to pull down the remaining avenue of trees which led off Greenbank Loan. The last tenant farmer at Greenbank, Dick Boa (whose family had run a wet dairy in Dorset Place), moved out to a sheep farm at West Linton.

Greenbank farmhouse and steadings formed an irregular-shaped rectangle on a north/south axis, enclosing a central courtyard. The entrance to the courtyard was on the north side, abutting Greenbank Loan. The steadings were in two sections, east and west, and the south end of the courtyard was closed by the two-storey, T-shaped farmhouse. The farmhouse had a walled and hedged garden to the south which was reached by a separate tree-lined driveway to the east of the steadings. To the west was an open yard where haystacks were built for the winter months. It is not known how old the buildings were but Greenbank is shown on maps of the area in the seventeenth century.

The residents of Greenbank were delighted with their new district, many having come from tenement flats in Morningside, Bruntsfield and Marchmont. There was a strong feeling of living in the country with very much more space and freedom, especially for children. Indeed, the building sites, with piles of stones and sand, made ideal playgrounds for the first few years. Temporary paths were laid by the builders, altered informally by the residents who were keen to find the quickest and easiest route to the tram cars on Pentland Terrace. Public transport was not ideal and most people did not own a car. There was no bus service on Greenbank Crescent which was not extended across the Braid Burn until the mid-1950s. The nearest tram service could only be reached by crossing what is now Braidburn Valley Park but there were no bridges over the burn. Considerable agility was required to negotiate the rudimentary stepping stones and planks before the residents were successful in petitioning for a bridge. As the number of houses increased, Edinburgh Corporation Transport Department decided to extend bus route No. 9 from its terminus at the top of Morningside Drive, via Morningside Grove and Greenbank Lane to a new terminus at the junction of Greenbank Road and Row. This service was introduced on 3rd January 1937 and was very popular, especially for those people living near the terminus who could remain in their houses until the bus arrived.

Most of the small access paths within the farm ground were lost, but others were created, notably running northwards from Greenbank Road to Greenbank Drive. The long 'ashy path' ran westwards from the farm steadings to about the position of No. 73 Greenbank Road. The only section of it to survive is the short lane leading to the City Hospital. Paths, for example between Greenbank Row and Rise, were considered but not implemented. The most historic pathway, now known as Fly Walk, was retained between Braidburn Valley Park and the gardens of the houses on the east side of the Crescent.

In the 1940s many advertisements referred to the War effort, including the purchase and construction of Anderson shelters. Courtesy of Edinburgh City Libraries.

Some things _must_ be done —

—but I drink McEWAN'S because I _like_ it !

EXPORT, PALE, AND STRONG ALES. William McEwan & Co Ltd Edinburgh

FLEMING'S STORES LTD.

For all reliable A.R.P. Equipment

AIR RAID SHELTERS

made from extra strong corrugated steel, suitable for erection in garden. To seat 6 persons; Size 5 ft. × 4 ft., £4. To seat 12 persons; Size 10 ft. × 4 ft., £6. EXTRAS—Double door at one end, 14/- Hinged shutters, 10/- SAND BAGS . . per dozen, 3/6

The Household Ironmongers

2 and 4 EARL GREY STREET

44 HOME STREET, EDINBURGH
259-261 ST. JOHN'S ROAD, CORSTORPHINE

Greenbank was more or less completed before the outbreak of the Second World War in 1939. In that year the War Office implemented a programme for the protection of the public in the event of an attack from the air. Special sirens, on the top of police boxes, produced an eerie, rising and falling, sound to warn the public of impending danger. To augment the sirens in outlying areas, wardens were appointed whose duty it was to alert the residents by sounding a clacker board and blowing a whistle in the street. This usually resulted in people coming out of their houses and looking up at the sky to see what was coming. What should have happened was that people should have taken cover, either in the cellars of their own houses, or, alternatively, in an Anderson Shelter specially constructed in the back garden.

In the early part of 1939 the Home Office issued several reports on 'Sectional Steel Shelters' which later came to be known as Anderson

James 'Ian' Stewart of Stewart & Co., Seedsmen, No. 13 South St Andrew Street, and his second daughter, Moyra, at No. 122 Greenbank Crescent in 1940. Note that the window is protected, against enemy action, by a timber frame loaded with sandbags, and covered by a mesh tarpaulin. *Courtesy of Mrs Sheila Bulmer, née Stewart.*

After nearly sixty years a few Anderson shelters still exist in Greenbank and other districts, but they are now used as garden sheds, 1998. *Courtesy of Catriona and Chris Ronald.*

Shelters after Sir John Anderson, the then Home Secretary. When the name 'Anderson Shelter' became popular, Sir John issued a long press statement to the effect that credit should go to the Air Raid Precautions Department who developed the design from an idea by William Paterson (later Sir William) of the Paterson Engineering Company. In addition to the formal reports, the Ministry of Home Security issued a short booklet entitled *Your Anderson Shelter this Winter* to help the public in their understanding of its benefits. Sixty years later its phraseology is almost humorous despite the seriousness of the situation at the time:

> A hammer, some nails and a saw, and possibly a pair of pliers that will cut wire are all the tools you will need ... Look at the diagram of the arrangement of bunks and you will at once see the idea ... Fix your canvas, hessian, wire netting etc., across the bunk frames,

Edinburgh Corporation Transport double-decker bus 225, registration number
HSG 175 (A.E.C. Regent Mark III, with Brockhouse body) at the terminus of the
No. 9 service at Greenbank Row, waiting for the return journey to Silverknowes
in September 1955. The No. 9 service had been extended to Greenbank Row
from the top end of Morningside Drive on 3rd January 1937 and was renumbered
39 from Sunday 23rd October 1955. On 8th February 1959 service No. 39 was
diverted to a new terminus, in Greenbank Drive, near the City Hospital.
Photograph by Alastair G. Gunn.

and the job is finished. Your local Council may be able to help
you to obtain the timber.

Never have a coke or other brazier in your shelter. It gives off
dangerous fumes ... If you need extra warmth, the best way to
secure it is a hot-water bottle, or a hot brick in your bed ... Put
your bricks in a hot oven, or in front of the fire for two hours, to
get thoroughly hot. An improvised heater can be made with two
large flowerpots and a candle. Fix the candle in one of the pots

and place it on the ground ... Light the candle and invert the
second flowerpot on top of the first.

Take with you: identity cards, ration books, gas masks, hot
drinks, shaded torch ... and a tin of biscuits in case the children
wake up hungry in the night.

Many Anderson Shelters were constructed in the back gardens of houses
in Greenbank which were used by residents during air raid alerts. At
least one enterprising resident built an air raid shelter of heavy timber
and sand bags, to accommodate up to eight people, in the corner of his
study at the rear of a bungalow in Greenbank Road. Very few people,
however, spent the whole night in one, as the district was never subject
to any sustained attack from the air. At the end of the Second World
War the shelters were dismantled but one, at least, has survived in a
back garden in Greenbank Road.

The 'C' Company of the 3rd Edinburgh Home Guard was set up on
25th May 1940 at the Golfers' Rest, Braid Hills from where it maintained constant watch throughout the war years. By 1944 when its
services were no longer required the men formed the Fairmilehead
Home Guard Club which met in the stables of Comiston House, then
occupied as the Pentland Hills Hotel. The history of the Company, *The
Watch on the Braids,* was written shortly after the war ended.

CHAPTER FOUR

Comiston Springs; Comiston House and Comiston Farm; Braidburn Valley Park

Comiston estate, which incorporated Comiston Farm, lay to the south of Greenbank, sharing a boundary along the south end of Braidburn Valley Park. It is an area of great historical interest for a number of reasons. Edinburgh's first piped water supply came from Comiston Springs in the seventeenth century as a result of an Act of the Scottish Parliament in 1621. A few hundred yards to the south of the springs was the sixteenth-century Comiston Castle, a small remnant of which still remains near Comiston House. The house dates from 1815 and has recently been restored as private residences. A lot of the open country-side of Comiston estate has obviously been built on but fortunately several wooded areas remain. Braidburn Valley Park, on the Greenbank estate, was created in the 1930s as a public park 'in all time coming'.

The housing developments of Comiston Springs were completed mainly by James Miller & Partners, the house builders. From 1935 to 1937 several applications were made for houses to be built in Comiston Springs Avenue and Pentland Crescent, Gardens and Grove. Miller returned in the 1950s and early 1960s to complete further housing.

COMISTON SPRINGS

In the sixteenth century, the population of Edinburgh was around 10,000 people, all of whom lived and worked in a comparatively small area between the Castle and the Canongate. Sanitary conditions were primitive, caused, in part, by a very inadequate supply of clean, germ-free water. One of the main sources was the Burgh or South Loch (now occupied by the Meadows) which was also used for a variety of un-hygienic practices such as washing dirty linen and watering herds of cattle. Maitland, writing in 1753, states that: 'The *Edinburghers* in the year 1621, having formed a Design, to bring sweet Water from the country, to supply themselves in the City with that precious Element, applied to Parliament for a Power to enable them to accomplish so desirable and necessary a Work'. Although there was no delay in getting the authority, it was not until 1672 that any real progress was made with the scheme.

The idea of a gravity-fed system, from Comiston Springs, was devised by George Sinclare, schoolmaster, mathematician, theologian and author of *Satan's Invisible World Discovered*. The contract, which was placed with a German engineer by the name of Peter Brauss or Bruschi, was to lay a 3-inch diameter lead pipe, a distance of nearly four miles, from Comiston to Castlehill in Edinburgh. For its day, it was a considerable feat of engineering, based on the premise that Comiston Springs lay at an altitude higher than Castlehill. In fact, Sinclare had calculated that Comiston was 60 feet higher than the proposed collecting tank at Castlehill. At the Comiston Springs end there was one spring in use to begin with but this was soon increased to four, each of which was connected to a collecting cistern at a slightly lower level. The original springs were named Tod, Hare, Swan and Tewchat or Peesweep: over the years Tod became Fox and Tewchat or Peesweep became Peewit. At one time, small lead animals, now at Huntly House Museum in the Canongate, were placed in the cistern to mark the outflow from each spring. The 3-inch pipe ran all the way to Castlehill, at a depth of one foot, via Braidburn Valley, the Hermitage of Braid, the Grange, Marchmont, Lauriston and the Grassmarket, culminating in a lead tank or reservoir at the head of Castlehill. From there it supplied five public wells situated at 'the Weigh House, the head of Forrester's Wynd, the Market Cross, the head of Niddry's Wynd, and the Nether Bow'. Other wells were added as demand grew, but the supply at Castlehill was never more than 210 Scots pints per minute.

By the early years of the eighteenth century, increases in the demand for water resulted in further serious shortages, requiring an increase in the diameter of the Comiston Springs pipe from 3 inches to 5 inches. This time the engineer was Desagulier and the contractor was Covay, who did not finish the work until 1720 – at least he thought he had finished the work but at the grand opening at Castlehill not a drop of water came out of the open valve. Covay left the reception party in great haste and rode furiously out to Comiston Springs to see what had gone wrong. Finding no explanation, he fled to Berwick rather than suffer the embarrassment of having to face the City Fathers, who, by that time, were probably past the stage of caring about adding any more water! The story goes that one of Covay's men realised that an air lock had occurred in the system and restored the flow by piercing the pipe with a nail. It is not recorded how the employee knew, at such short notice, where the air lock was, nor how such an elementary explanation could have escaped Covay himself. However, an article in *The Scots Magazine* in 1760 mentions some of the practical difficulties of a gravity-fed system over such a long distance. Eventually there were thirteen air cocks or valves fitted 'on the eminences of the ground', which were all opened when the water was first released at Comiston. When the water reached the valves, they were successively closed, thus ensuring that no air was left in each section of the pipe. In addition to

Water Caddie
Edinburgh

Edinburgh's early water caddies carried water in barrels on their back, secured by a leather strap, usually to their right forearm. Most people fetched their own water from the public wells but those who could afford to pay one penny per barrel or stoup used the services of a caddie. *From* The Edinburgh and District Water Supply.

Waiting at the Wells Edinburgh

There were frequent interruptions of supply at the public wells, and often there were arguments between the water caddies and members of the public. In the picture the traditional water stoup is being filled; two were carried at once, attached to a wooden gird round the body of the caddie. *From* The Edinburgh and District Water Supply.

that, there were four cleansing cocks in the low-lying sections which could be opened from time to time to wash out silt deposits and keep the pipe clear.

There was a lot of controversy, and threatened legal action, between the City and the Laird of Comiston over the level of compensation to be paid for the extraction of the water. Exactly what sums were paid is not now clear but the annual wayleave, or feu, required the Magistrates and Town Council to provide the Lady of Comiston with the best silk gown it was in the power of the Corporation to bestow, and to pay to the proprietor the sum of 7/6d (37p) per annum.

For many years Edinburgh's first piped water supply came from Comiston
Springs. The photograph shows the interior of the collecting cistern, which still
exists to the south of Oxgangs Avenue. The lead animals (Hare, Fox, Swan and
Peewit), which marked the outflow of each spring, are now in Huntly House
Museum in the Canongate. *From* The Water Supply of Edinburgh.

Needless to say, Comiston Springs was never going to be able to
supply the steadily increasing demands for more water. In 1760 a new
7-inch pipe was laid from Swanston which yielded an additional 200,000
gallons each day into two iron tanks in Edinburgh Castle. When the
Edinburgh Water Company was formed in 1819, it took over all the
pipes and cisterns for the sum of £30,000. One of its first tasks was the
construction of Glencorse Reservoir and the collection of water from
the Crawley Springs. The water, partly in pipes 18 inches in diameter
and partly 15 inches, was brought to Edinburgh in 1821, in an almost
level gradient, boosting the daily supply to 2,500,000 gallons. After the
1821 improvements, some houses in the Old Town were fitted with
individual supplies, but, for the most part, people still went to the public
wells to carry water, unless they could afford to pay one of the water
carriers, or caddies, one penny per stoup. Collecting water was very
much part of the social scene. The supply was usually available only at
night and was on a strict 'first come, first served' basis, i.e. for the
members of the public, but the caddies gave themselves authority to

jump the queue. They were considered to be a rather rough lot, males and females, whose attempt at self-regulation 'imposed' by the Magistrates was undermined by their natural enthusiasm to outdo one another in matters of vulgarity and coarseness. Householders would leave their receptacles in line at the well and congregate later when the supply was on. James Colston, author of *The Edinburgh and District Water Supply*, 1890, observed that all manner of vessels were used, including washing tubs, pails, stoups, tea kettles, pans, jugs and pitchers 'and even articles of still commoner use'. In an attempt to reduce the friction between the caddies and the public, some wells were fitted with two outlets, one of which had a stone fitted to take the bilge, or base, of the standard water stoup, used by the caddies. At one time the caddies carried the water in a barrel on their backs, but the more common method was two stoups on either side of a wooden gird round the body of the carrier. The standard stoup was made of wood, girded by four iron hoops, 24 inches high, circular, broad at the bottom and narrow at the top. They became something of a doubtful status symbol when chosen as a wedding present: the custom was that the groom would present his young bride with a beautiful set of stoups upon their marriage, thus emphasising whose task it would be to fetch the water. The tradition of 'weeting the stoups' was the last bachelor act performed by the groom and his friends on what would nowadays be called a 'stag night'.

Between 1819 and 1869 various schemes were implemented to increase the supply of water from the north side of the Pentland Hills. This necessitated the construction of compensating reservoirs to maintain the water level in the River Almond and the Water of Leith, both of which still had many water-powered mill wheels. In 1869 the Edinburgh Water Company was replaced by the Edinburgh & District Water Trust which was responsible for the Moorfoot scheme in the 1870s and Talla in 1905. Comiston Springs ceased to feed the town's water supply in 1946 because of the danger of contamination from surrounding houses, but, by then, its percentage contribution was very small. Today, Edinburgh's supply from the Pentland Hills, Talla, Moorfoot, Fruid and Megget schemes is filtered at Rosebery, Torduff, Marchbank, Fairmilehead and Alnwickhill in a complicated system far removed from the first supply at Comiston Springs, planned in 1621.

Several reminders of the first scheme still exist. At Comiston the collecting cistern stands in open ground to the west of Swan Spring

Avenue and the wellheads are marked by protective masonry in and around the grounds of Hunter's Tryst School. At Castlehill the old reservoir was taken out of use many years ago and is now occupied by the Edinburgh Old Town Weaving Company which has an exhibition and a working tartan weaving mill. Perhaps the most unusual feature, which is frequently associated, wrongly, with hostilities at the Castle, is the cannonball which is embedded in the gable wall of Cannonball House, immediately opposite the Weaving Company. High up on the west gable is a small cannonball set into the masonry, looking very much like a shot from the ramparts. The cannonball was inserted at a height of 329 feet above sea level or 60 feet lower than Comiston Springs, thus ensuring that the water would be able to flow, by gravity, from Comiston to the Old Town.

COMISTON HOUSE AND COMISTON FARM

According to *The Place Names of Edinburgh* by Stuart Harris, the name Comiston is recorded from the year 1337. Mr Harris states that 'The early spellings *Colemanstone* and *Colemanstoun* show the name to be Anglian *Colman's Tún*, the farm belonging to someone bearing the name of Colman'. In relation to modern street names, the farm was bounded: on the east by Braid Road and Buckstone Terrace; on the south by Oxgangs Road; on the west by Oxgangs Park, Rise and Avenue; and on the north by the south end of Braidburn Valley Park. The Buck Stone, in Braid Road, marked the junction of four estates: Comiston, Greenbank, Braid and Mortonhall.

The centre of the Comiston estate was Comiston Castle, believed to date from the sixteenth century, a small portion of which still remains to the east of Cockmylane. The old castle was superseded by Comiston House, built in 1815, and now restored as private flats at the west end of Camus Avenue. Several leading families, including Foulis, Fairlie, Creich, Cant, Porterfield and Forrest, have been associated with Comiston Castle and House over the centuries.

Comiston was owned by James Foulis of Colinton in 1531, followed by John Fairlie at the end of the sixteenth century and then by Andrew Creich and his wife Margaret Dick in 1608. Their son was also Andrew Creich, whose daughter Catherine Creich acquired the estate in 1631 with her husband John Cant of the Grange of St Giles. The property

William Wilkie, farmer, and his daughter, Isla, and the family dog, Dick, at the
front door of Braid Farmhouse, *c.* 1919. William Wilkie was tenant farmer at
Braid and Comiston. *Courtesy of Miss Isla Wilkie.*

came to the Porterfield family on the marriage of John Cant's daughter, Catherine Cant, to William Porterfield, and remained in the family until 1715 when Comiston entered one of its most interesting phases.

The long and distinguished association of the Forrest family with Comiston began in 1715 when the property was bought by James Forrest. The family came to prominence in the middle of the nineteenth century on the birth of a later James Forrest, who became a Writer to the Signet. When he married his cousin Catherine, only daughter and heir to the estate of Comiston, his future as a prominent landowner was assured. On his death in 1820 the estate passed to his heir, also James, who became Lord Provost of Edinburgh.

Sir James Forrest, 1st Baronet, born in 1780, was admitted as an advocate to the Scottish Bar in 1803. It was he who built the present Comiston House in 1815 towards the end of his father's life. He was an ambitious and able man who held a number of public and private appointments, including Grand Master Mason for Scotland from 1838 to 1840, and Lord Provost from 1838 to 1843. Being Lord Provost at the time of Queen Victoria's coronation, he was made a baronet in honour of that occasion. During his term of office he was deeply involved in many of the important issues of the day. Shortly after his election he called a meeting to petition Parliament for the adoption of voting by ballot to prevent intimidation. He became involved in pressure groups for the repeal of the Corn Laws (which imposed duty on imported cereals) and the abolition of patronage. His dislike of church patronage made him an obvious choice to lead the many members of the Town Council who joined the Free Church in 1843.

Despite his otherwise impeccable conduct, and a long list of civic accomplishments, few writers have been able to resist the temptation to recount his most inglorious moment. In 1842 Queen Victoria and Prince Albert visited Scotland shortly after the coronation. It was an occasion of great public jubilation with bonfires lit at various vantage points as the Royal Fleet made its way up the Forth. The following morning the Queen left the royal yacht a few minutes before nine o'clock to come ashore, but the Provost and his Town Council were under the impression that their presence would not be required until more than an hour later. Undaunted and unescorted, the young Queen proceeded with her itinerary, meeting the people and His Grace the Duke of Buccleuch who was one of the few dignitaries present. Needless to say, this unintentional *faux pas* created great merriment which was quickly set to verse in a parody of the Jacobite song *Hey, Johnny Cope*, the new version being:

> Hey, Jamie Forrest, are ye waukin' yet?
> Or are your Baillies snorin' yet?
> If you are waukin' I would wit
> Ye'd hae a merry, merry mornin'!
>
> The Queen she's come to Granton Pier,
> Nae Provost and nae Baillie here,
> They're in their beds I muckle fear,
> Sae early in the mornin'!

With characteristic Royal diplomacy the Queen announced that there had been a change in arrangements to accommodate a visit to Dalkeith Palace where the keys of the city were later presented to Her Majesty by Provost Forrest.

After the death of the Lord Provost in 1860 Comiston remained in the possession of the Forrest family for some years, but the Baronetcy became extinct in 1928 on the death of Sir Charles Forrest whose only son was killed in the First World War

Comiston Farm

Comiston Farm resisted urban development for much longer than Greenbank Farm. The large, square, stone-built farmhouse, set among mature trees to the west of Pentland View, has survived, but is no longer used as a private house. The ground floor consisted of a large drawing room to the front (to the left on entry), and a dining room to the right. Beyond the drawing room was a small parlour, and beyond the dining room was the butler's pantry (the walls of which were lined with shelves) and a small room used as an office. At the back of the house were the usual offices of kitchen, scullery, toilet, wash house, and a small stair leading to the maid's room. Upstairs, there was a bathroom, a dressing room and five bedrooms. The farm steadings, and farm labourers' cottages (now demolished) lay to the north, on the sloping ground between the farmhouse and the Braid Burn. A path, still known as Cockmylane, ran northwards to join up to Fly Walk which led to Greenbank Farm.

Comiston Farmhouse, *c.* 1947, when the house was occupied by the Harwell family. The steadings, to the right, were demolished many years ago but the farmhouse is still there. *Courtesy of George G. Harwell.*

William Wilkie and his wife Barbara Bethune, née Birrell, came from Fife to Braid Farm in 1916 as tenant farmers, and also took over responsibility for Comiston Farm from 1925 to 1937. The family, consisting of a son and two daughters, lived, firstly, at Braid Farm and then at Comiston Farm from 1926. Mr Wilkie also looked after a few fields at Greenbank Farm after the last tenant farmer, Dick Boa, had left, and the houses of Greenbank were encroaching. In the 1920s and '30s Comiston was a mixed farm, arable and dairy, with the addition of some pigs and bullocks kept for fattening. There was a herd of about eighty dairy cows (Braid and Comiston Farms) which were milked, by hand, twice a day, milking machinery being introduced later. The milk was sold in large pitchers to Fortune's Dairy at Dalhousie Terrace, and Gemmell's Dairy in Morningside Road, among others.

Before the days of mechanisation, there were about twelve employees, most of whom lived on or near the farm, plus itinerant workers brought in at particular times, for example at harvest or potato lifting. Their

The view south from Comiston Farm to Oxgangs Road and the T-woods,
c. 1947. The area is now built up but the path, on the left, known as
Cockmylane, survives. *Courtesy of George G. Harwell.*

weekly wages were modest, ranging downwards from the byreman
assisted by his daughters, the grieve, the foreman, the ploughmen, the
women workers and the orraman (odd-job man). The farmer's wife
derived a small income from selling eggs, either to passing trade or to
regular customers who called at the farmhouse for their orders. Eggs,
for home consumption, were kept fresh for several weeks during the
non-laying season by immersing them in isinglass, a purifying agent
made from the air bladders of freshwater fish.

The busiest times on the farm were, of course, bringing in the hay,
the harvest and the potato crop. After the hay was cut, it was left in
the field to dry before being brought into the yard for stacking. As the
corn stacks were taken down during the winter months, the last one
would be ringed with chicken wire a few feet from the base, and
two dogs would be put into the space between the stack and the
wire. When the startled rats tried to make their escape, they were
trapped by the wire and finished off by the dogs. At harvest time, Bert
Darling from Loanhead arrived with his power-driven threshing
machine which reduced greatly the physical effort needed to thresh the
corn, especially when assistance was given by neighbouring farms on a
reciprocal basis.

The farm workers' cottages at Comiston Farm in the mid-1950s, shortly before demolition for house building. *Courtesy of William Haggerty.*

George and Elizabeth Harwell took over the tenancy of Comiston Farm in 1938 and lived at the farmhouse until 1978. During their tenancy, mechanisation gradually reduced the workforce to only three men who lived in the farm cottages. Much of the farm remained intact until the mid-1950s when further feuing plans eventually brought housing right up to the farmhouse perimeter wall. The Harwells were also owners of Harwell's of Colinton, the stationer, newsagent, dairy, baker and tearoom in Bridge Road in Colinton.

BRAIDBURN VALLEY PARK

In 1933 the City of Edinburgh began negotiations with Mortonhall and Charterhall Estates for the purchase of approximately 28 acres of ground at Braidburn Valley, with a view to turning it into a public park. One of the proposed conditions was 'that the ground shall be kept as an open space for all time coming and shall only be used as a public park'. Its precipitous sides, and the presence of the burn and various water pipes, probably made it unsuitable for house-building in the 1930s.

Harvesting at Braidburn in 1910 when the land was still part of Greenbank Farm. The second cottage from the left is Greenbank Cottage, illustrated in Chapter 3. The next building is a temporary site hut for David Adamson of Morningside Road who is in the process of completing Nos. 1–7 Greenbank Crescent. The photograph, by R. A. Rayner, probably includes members of the Moggie family.

This photograph is taken from about the same position as the above but in the direction of the Braid Hills Hotel and Pentland Terrace. It is dated after 1903 but before 1909 and shows cable cars on the main road. *Courtesy of R. S. Russell.*

A moment's reflection at a quiet spot on the high path of what is now Braidburn Valley Park. The photograph, dated April 1924, is from the album of the late Miss Joanna Wilson, formerly of No. 11 Greenbank Crescent. *Courtesy of Allison Naismith and Ian Mitchell.*

Mother and son, and family pet, on the small pedestrian bridge (removed several years ago) over the Braid Burn at the west end of the Park. From the album of the late Miss Joanna Wilson. *Courtesy of Allison Naismith and Ian Mitchell.*

Marker stones, on the eastern slopes, show the position of the first water supply to the town from Comiston Springs. A 12-inch diameter pipe laid in 1908, and a 30-inch diameter pipe laid in 1922, traverse the park, carrying water eastwards from Firrhill to Comiston and Morningside. A deep sewer pipe also runs the length of the park near the course of the Braid Burn.

Shortly after the park was first opened, the north entrance was greatly enhanced by the erection of stone pillars with iron gates incorporating the initials of King George VI and Queen Elizabeth. The gates and pillars had previously stood at the entrance lodge to Comiston House. In 1923 when Comiston Road (Buckstone Terrace) was being widened, near present-day Camus Avenue, the gates and pillars were moved back about three metres and some minor alterations were made to the lodge. Little did the authorities know that within a fairly short time the pillars would be on the move again to their present site.

On the afternoon of Saturday, 2nd November 1935, five thousand Girl Guides, Rangers and Brownies assembled in the park to plant 400 cherry trees, as a gift to the City, in honour of the Silver Jubilee of King George V. The King did not attend the event, but his message was read out to the assembled audience by Lord Provost Sir William J. Thomson, who received the gift on behalf of the City from Miss Dalmahoy, the County Commissioner. After the Lord Provost had planted the first tree, there was a great deal of activity as the girls proceeded to plant the other 399 before it got dark! Most of the trees have survived, providing spectacular flowering in the spring, but the labels, giving details of the companies involved, have long since become detached from the trees. The small commemorative plaques have also disappeared.

The inauguration of the 'Braidburn Valley Scheme' was also marked in June 1937 as part of the Coronation celebrations for King George VI. A thousand school children gave a massed display of dancing and gymnastics before an audience of 3,000. The open-air theatre had just been opened, providing a stage on the east side, and a terraced arena for the audience on the west side. A special platform was brought in, measuring 150 feet by 60 feet, to accommodate the highlight of the show – the Rose Dance which had previously been performed before Queen Mary at Holyrood in July 1934.

During the years of the Second World War, much of the ground at the north end of the park was dug up for allotments, which were still

Daniel Moggie at his allotment at Braidburn in 1944. Daniel knew the soil well, having been the grieve at Greenbank Farm until his retirement in 1926. *Courtesy of Dan Moggie.*

being tended in the 1960s. In the 1940s, however, the allotment holder
who must surely have had the greatest 'claim of right' was Daniel
Moggie, who had cultivated the same soil when he was grieve at Greenbank Farm before his retirement in 1926.

At the end of the Second World War, the open-air theatre was used
by several drama groups and opera companies, with great success,
despite the vagaries of the weather. In June 1945 the Phillip Barrett
Company did *A Midsummer Night's Dream* as part of a Shakespearean
Festival, attended, on the opening night, by the Lord and Lady Provost.
This was followed by *As You Like It* which attracted 10,000 people in
the first three days, and finally *The Merchant of Venice*, which included
a performance by the Jean Reynolds School of Dancing. *The Scotsman*
commented particularly on the experiment of playing Shakespeare in
the open air:

A scene from *Merrie England* performed by the Southern Light Opera Company
at the Open-Air Theatre in Braidburn Valley Park in June 1946. *Courtesy of
David McBain.*

'Early Spring in the Braidburn' by the artist Joseph Milne (1861–1911). *Courtesy of Sotheby's Picture Library.*

... though the company was thoroughly competent, defects were bound to intrude in a wide amphitheatre such as that at Braidburn Park. The microphone leads to a certain distortion of the natural voice, and with a veering wind the actors' speech seems to come alternately from different quarters. A sudden gust, moreover, has the effect of producing a sound something like thunder ... The music and the singing were particularly delightful out of doors.

In the summer of 1946 at least three other companies came to Braidburn Park, including the Edinburgh and Lothians Districts of the Scottish Community Drama Association who did *Rob Roy* and the Bohemian Lyric Opera Company with *A Country Girl*. The Southern Light Opera Company performed *Merrie England* during the first week of June 1946, the director, Fraser Neal, treating the opera on the lines of a pageant and using the entire area as a stage. The City Parks Department entered

Braidburn Valley Park – ever popular with children and adults alike. The gates and pillars were brought from the former entrance to Comiston House when the Park was first opened.
Photograph by Phyllis M. Cant

into the spirit of the occasion by providing shrubs and flowers for the stage, and damming the Braid Burn to provide a sufficient depth of water for Queen Elizabeth to make her triumphal entry by Royal Barge. By all accounts the weather played it cool: 'A valiant orchestra, led by Dr John Fairbairn and conducted by Mr R. W. Creswell defied the falling thermometer in the only proper way by playing all the more vigorously'. Later in the week, the thermometer and the barometer fell so low that the Wednesday performance was cancelled. Undeterred, the Southern Light Opera Company returned to Braidburn in June 1947 as part of their fiftieth anniversary and performed *The Vagabond King* in very similar conditions. Following the Tuesday evening performances, the gales increased to such an extent that the scenery was badly damaged.

The Southern Light Opera Company was formed on 6th March 1897 at a meeting in the Union Hotel, Cockburn Street, Edinburgh. To mark its centenary, a history of the Company, by David McBain, was published in 1997 under the title *More a Way of Life*, which includes several references to the Braidburn performances.

In more recent years, the park has hosted sheepdog trials, dog shows, and various performances from the Edinburgh Festival. In 1998 the City of Edinburgh Council commissioned a feasibility study to establish an arboretum in Braidburn Valley Park. The existing trees include a mature row of Wheatley elms parallel to Pentland Terrace.

CHAPTER FIVE

City Poorhouse; Greenlea; The Steils; City Hospital; Merchants of Edinburgh Golf Club; South Morningside Primary School

The western boundary of Greenbank Farm was along the line of the back gardens on the west side of Greenbank Road. To the west of that line two important institutions were built on land which had previously been open countryside. In 1870 Edinburgh's Charity Workhouse moved from its antiquated premises in Forrest Road to the new City Poorhouse, built on part of the Lands of Craiglockhart. Over the years it has changed its name, and its emphasis, firstly to Glenlockhart, and then to Greenlea. In the 1980s Greenlea Old People's Home was closed and the site redeveloped as The Steils by Miller Homes of Edinburgh.

Also in the nineteenth century, the Town Council was anxious to find a site for a new fever hospital to remedy the appalling lack of proper facilities for the treatment of infectious diseases like cholera and smallpox. After several sites had been considered, the new City Hospital was built 'at Colinton Mains', and opened in 1903. Unfortunately, the city's fever hospital is now scheduled for closure, and the site will be redeveloped (retaining most of the original buildings) by Morrison Homes.

Another large tract of land, part of the Lands of Craiglockhart, was laid out in 1907 by the Merchants of Edinburgh Golf Club who have recently renewed a long lease, ensuring that the ground will be used as a golf course for many years to come.

The last item in this chapter is South Morningside Primary School in Comiston Road, opened in 1892 as a replacement for the tiny 'village' school in Morningside Road, opposite the junction with Falcon Avenue.

THE CITY POORHOUSE; GREENLEA OLD PEOPLE'S HOME; THE STEILS

In the middle of the nineteenth century, Edinburgh's Charity Workhouse was housed in two very old buildings on either side of Forrest Road. The east wing was in the triangle formed by Teviot Place, Bristo Place and Forrest Road, which, at one time, had housed the infamous City Bedlam for 'lunatic paupers', where the poet, Robert Fergusson, had died in 1774. The west wing was to the east of Greyfriars Kirk.

In September 1861 a *Report by the House Committee of the Parochial Board of Edinburgh as to New Poorhouse Accommodation* was published, drawing attention to the overcrowding at the Workhouse and the difficulties of trying to expand the site. The Board considered closing Forrest Road (which had only been opened about twenty years earlier) but rejected the idea on the basis that 'it forms such a necessary communication between the City and the Southern Districts, that the shutting of it up would be felt to be a public loss'. The *Report* went on to say that even if the Forrest Road land had become available there would still be insufficient space and 'the fatuous poor would still require

Officials at the Peace Celebrations on 30th July 1919 when the Merchants of Edinburgh Golf Club entertained the inmates of Edinburgh City Poorhouse. *Courtesy of the Merchants of Edinburgh Golf Club.*

to be accommodated elsewhere'. In 1861 the Forrest Road premises were designed to accommodate 580 inmates (male and female) but actually held 622. The Board came to the view that new premises were needed to house 700 ordinary inmates, plus 200 'fatuous', at an estimated cost of £30,500, with provision for a later increase to 1,000 ordinary inmates. That view, forcibly put to a meeting of ratepayers in Messrs Smith & Philpot's Rooms at No. 79 George Street, was fully reported by *The Scotsman*: '. . . the wisest, cheapest, and best course for the parish to follow is to obtain a sufficient quantity of ground out of the city on which to erect buildings to accommodate the ordinary paupers, and the fatuous and incurable'.

A design competition was opened in 1865 shortly after land had been purchased at Craiglockhart for £29,000. The winner, George Beattie, envisaged a range of stone buildings, in the Scottish baronial style, at an estimated cost of £41,000. In September 1865 Mr Beattie prepared a very full report, with supporting plans and drawings, under the title *New City Poorhouse at Craiglockhart*. The introductory paragraphs highlighted the philosophy of the day by confirming that the new Poorhouse 'should furnish a cheerful and comfortable abode . . . for the poor, aged and infirm, helpless and/or insane'. It also stated:

> There are others, however; the dissipated, the improvident, and the vicious, who are only too ready to enter the Poorhouse, and throw the burden of their responsibility upon the community. For these a stricter and more rigorous discipline is necessary so that the Poorhouse may act as a test of real poverty, and not become a place where the lazy and the vicious are maintained in idleness. To render the Poorhouse unattractive to such, an entire separation of classes, a strict discipline, and a constant surveillance are indispensable.

Males and females were strictly separated, except in the dining room and the chapel. Even in the dining room, the men were kept to the west side, separated from the women on the other side by 'a low screen, not too high so as to injure the appearance of the hall or give it a prisonlike appearance'.

The layout was basically a series of pavilions arranged around a central clock tower. The central block contained the reception hall and the chaplain's room, behind which were the dining room and the kitchens. The west wing was for men, with a nomenclature all of its own: on the ground floor, day room for old men of doubtful character; infirm men's ward; dissolute men's day room; lunatics' dayroom. Separate airing grounds were provided for each classification. The first floor was occupied by the paupers' clothes stores, the venereal ward and the itch ward. The remainder of the first floor, and all the second floor, were given over to dormitories with the same classifications as the ground floor. Much the same arrangements were applied to the women in the east wing, which also contained children. There was also a separate dayroom for infants under five years of age. When inmates first arrived, they were placed in probationary wards to await assessment.

The north-west corner of the complex (near the highest point of Glenlockhart Road) contained a farmyard surrounded by the stick shed, byre, straw house, turnip shed and loose box. The adjacent stable yard had numerous stalls, a gig shed (one van horse for communication with Edinburgh), and a fire engine. The range of workshops included the carpenter's shop, the plumber's shop, the smith's shop and the shoe-maker's shop. Further evidence of the institution's independence was found in the north-east corner which contained a laundry, washing house, drying house and bleaching green, as well as a bakehouse, bread store and flour store.

The infirmary was situated on the extreme east side of the grounds with a central administrative block, flanked by female wards on the west side and male wards on the east side. Before deciding on the size of the wards, Mr Beattie took cognisance of the very best advice available by referring to Miss Nightingale's evidence to the Army Sanitary Commission: 'The best size of ward, for ensuring the two conditions of health and facility of discipline, is from twenty to thirty-two sick'. Separate from the infirmary, and further to the east, was a small block containing a mortuary, coffin house, post mortem room and dressing room.

The foundation stone for the new City Poorhouse was laid by the Grand Master of the Orange Order of Masons on 4th July 1867. The official opening was on 2nd May 1870, but, before then, serious problems arose concerning an adequate supply of fresh water. In 1870 Craiglockhart was well outside the Edinburgh city boundary, as a result of which the Edinburgh Water Company was not empowered to supply water, even although it was keen to do so. The Edinburgh Parish

Poorhouse Water Supply Act received the Royal Assent on 24th June 1869, enabling the Edinburgh Water Company to lay a pipe, not exceeding 6 inches in diameter, from their Swanston pipe near Hunter's Tryst, through the lands of Comiston, Oxgangs and Colinton Mains, terminating in the central tower of the Poorhouse building. The supply was to be metered at a cost of 6d (2½p) per thousand imperial gallons, and the Company was not bound to supply more than 20,000 gallons in any one day 'unless they have it in their power conveniently to do so'. Early maps also indicate that a natural water supply was drawn from springs on Easter Craiglockhart Hill and was pumped into the Poorhouse buildings from the north side of Glenlockhart Road.

When the Poorhouse was first opened, it was a long way from Edinburgh's public transport system. There were two main approaches, one from the west, along what is now Glenlockhart Road, and the other from the east, off Comiston Road. There were three lodges, sometimes referred to as East Lodge, Mid Lodge (or Middle Lodge), and West Lodge. East Lodge was on the west side of Comiston Road, immediately

The Edinburgh City Poorhouse East Lodge was demolished in 1987 to make way for the construction of Greenbank House in Comiston Road.

north of present-day Greenbank Drive. The Poorhouse Drive ran west-wards from East Lodge, along the line of the trees which lie between the north side of Greenbank Drive and the back gardens of the houses on the south side of Comiston Drive. East Lodge, demolished in 1987 for the construction of Greenbank House, had the address No. 144 Comiston Road, which, for many years, was the address shown on the birth certificates of those children unfortunate enough to have been born in the City Poorhouse. Mid, or Middle, Lodge was on the north side of Glenlockhart Road about midway between the Poorhouse build-ings and the junction with Colinton Road and Craiglockhart Avenue. On the *Plan of Lands at Craiglockhart*, dated 1880, it is described as 'Gatehouse', the gate across the road being a few yards to the west of the lodge. Mid Lodge is described as 'Lodge' in the *Ordnance Survey Maps* of 1895, 1908, 1914 and 1932. The 1968 *Ordnance Survey Map* refers to it as Middle Lodge, even although the Dean of Guild approved its demolition on 13th May 1966. When Middle Lodge was demolished, part of the front wall was retained, on which there is a bench mark. West Lodge, or West Cottage, still exists at the point where Glenlock-hart Road narrows to the east of the remains of Craiglockhart Castle. It is not nearly as old as Middle Lodge or East Lodge: it appears for the first time on the 1932 *Ordnance Survey Map* but does not appear on the 1914 *Map*. West Lodge retains stone gate piers, on either side of the road, confirming that it was also a gatehouse.

During both World Wars part of the City Poorhouse was used to accommodate a small military hospital. By the end of the Second World War the complex was renamed Glenlockhart, and in 1964 it became Greenlea Old People's Home. All the buildings then existing were included in a plan, dated January 1960, drawn by the City Architect's Department, on which the layout of the former Poorhouse was still evident, i.e. the administrative block in the centre, the men's residences on the west side, the women's residences on the east, and the old infirmary partly used for sick wards. However, the regime, and the old rules and phraseology had changed out of all recognition. Greenlea was closed in the late 1980s and the entire site was purchased by Miller Homes for a new housing development.

Many memories of the City Poorhouse and Greenlea remain, both from people who lived there and people from the surrounding districts who were involved in the work being done. Several Greenbank families

Part of the attractive housing development created in the 1990s by Miller Homes in the buildings and grounds of Edinburgh's former City Poorhouse. *Photograph by Phyllis M. Cant.*

used to attend Mass on Sunday mornings in a little chapel on the east side of the buildings. The priest was Father John McGrain, attached to St Cuthbert's Parish at Slateford, who had spent much of his time in Pakistan with St Joseph's Missionary Society before returning to Britain, on account of ill-health. As Father McGrain was chaplain to the Poorhouse and other hospitals on the south side of the city, he lived, for convenience, in Greenbank Terrace where his sisters, the Misses McGrain, kept house for him. The chapel finally closed for worship during the Second World War. After the last Mass, the father of a young family was entrusted with the task of carrying the chalice back to Father McGrain's house at Greenbank Terrace. The priest wrapped the chalice in linen, then in silk, then in layers of brown paper for the short journey. In an endeavour to instil the appropriate degree of solemnity, the children were forbidden by their father to speak during the journey. Many

The Clock Tower of the former Edinburgh City Poorhouse (later Greenlea) which now forms a central part of The Steils constructed by Miller Homes. *Photograph by Phyllis M. Cant.*

years later, when one of the children revisited the Poorhouse as an adult, she asked to see the old chapel, which, by then, had become the tailor's shop. In the course of conversation, the tailor admitted that he did not know what was behind the sealed door opposite the entrance – but the visitor had no difficulty in recalling: it had been the confessional in the original chapel.

The Greenlea site, with certain exceptions at the south-west corner, was purchased by Miller Homes in 1988 for residential development. The five original blocks, centred on the clock tower, were completely refurbished, and the more recent interconnecting buildings were demolished, allowing extra windows to be opened on the exposed gable walls. To the north of the clock tower, all the buildings, which had previously been used as the dining room, kitchens, stables, workshops and laundry, were demolished. Around 220 houses and flats were constructed in four separate developments, all named after the fields on which the City Poorhouse had been built. The Steils has the original buildings on its north side and a line of new detached houses on the south side. Mid Steil lies to the north of The Steils, flanked by Wester Steil and Easter Steil. Wester Steil is built on ground previously used, in part, as a vegetable garden and Easter Steil includes the conversion of the old infirmary blocks. Planning, demolition and reconstruction took ten years from first acquisition. The overall result is an excellent combination of the old and the new, retaining the best features of the old City Poorhouse and introducing new buildings with a distinctly traditional appearance of crowsteps, finials and ironwork. South Steil, developed independently of Miller Homes, lies in the south-west corner of the estate.

THE CITY HOSPITAL

Edinburgh suffered serious outbreaks of cholera in 1832, and again in 1849, at a time when the city was ill-equipped to deal with the ravages of infectious diseases. Chronic overcrowding, and a lack of basic hygiene in the tenements of the Old Town, provided the ideal environment for the spread of disease. Despite numerous protestations from the more enlightened citizens of the day, it was not until 1862 that Edinburgh appointed its first Medical Officer of Health, Dr (later Sir) Henry Littlejohn of the Department of Medical Jurisprudence in Edinburgh's Medical School. One of Dr Littlejohn's first tasks was his *Report on the Sanitary Condition of the City of Edinburgh*, published in 1865, in which he commented, 'Disease is spreading like wildfire in houses without proper running water and flush toilets'. In response, the Town Council purchased Canongate Poorhouse in 1867 for £1,600 and converted it into a fever hospital. This work was continued at the new Royal Infirmary when it was opened at Lauriston in 1879. However, there was a setback in 1885 when the Royal Infirmary informed the Town Council that it could no longer accommodate patients with infectious diseases. As a result, the wards were transferred to the site of the old Infirmary building in Infirmary Street. This unsatisfactory state of affairs came to a head in 1894 when the Old Infirmary site could not cope with an outbreak of smallpox, requiring some patients to be admitted to 'large wooden structures' in Holyrood Park.

If nothing else, the 1894 outbreak of smallpox acted as a catalyst for a more comprehensive approach to the problem. Dr Littlejohn's quest for a completely new fever hospital was at last being talked about, and the Town Council began a series of consultations with the Royal College of Physicians of Edinburgh. After all the arguments had been considered, it was decided that the new hospital should be located outside the city, rather than in any piecemeal development of a city-centre site. On the question of accessibility, the committee were obviously influenced by the finding that 'ambulance waggons are now so constructed that fever patients can be carried in them over considerable distances without serious risk'.

Various sites were considered, including seventeen acres at Grange Terrace, along with the house known as South Park, which was latterly used by the British Geological Survey. A much larger site, extending to thirty acres, on the eastern slope of the Blackford Hill 'to the south of the road leading from the Harrison Arch', was also seen as a serious contender. It is difficult to see why either of these sites warranted so much consideration when they were only a fraction of the size of the ground eventually secured. Colinton Mains Farm was bought by the Town Council for £20,000, providing 130 acres, of which 72 acres were set aside for the new hospital. The City Architect, Robert Morham, was instructed to draw up plans for a fever hospital, capable (on the advice of Dr Littlejohn) of accommodating 600 patients. The ceremony of 'cutting the first sod' was undertaken in May 1897 by Lady Mc-Donald, in the presence of her husband, Lord Provost Sir Andrew McDonald.

Mr Morham's remit was well documented in an account, dated 1903, by W. Lang Todd, Convener of the Public Health Committee. The chosen site was almost completely clear of existing buildings and had an uninterrupted view of the Pentland Hills, a mile and a half to the south. The gentle south-facing slope was to be fully exploited by building a series of two-storey pavilion blocks, sufficiently far apart not to overshadow one another. The entire range of buildings was to be constructed of light red-coloured stone 'warmer and pleasanter [in appearance] than much of the stone in common use in the "grey metropolis of the north"'.

One principal entrance was planned on the north side. On the left of the entrance gate was the porter's lodge, and further in, on the right, the Medical Superintendent's house. The centre block was occupied by general offices with the nurses' and servants' homes behind. The main ward pavilions were laid out in double rows to the east and west. Those on the east side, accounting for more than half the hospital's original capacity, were for cases of scarlet fever (327 beds); and those on the west side dealt with cases of diphtheria, typhoid, erysipelas, measles, chicken-pox, whooping cough and typhus. There were also small isolation wards to the east and west for patients whose diagnosis was not yet complete. The eastern section of the site (nearest to the present-day district of Greenbank) contained an education block for students and nurses, the chapel, the mortuary and the laundry. Most of the separate pavilions were linked by a system of covered passages which enabled staff and patients to move from one part of the hospital to another with, at least, some protection from the elements. Below the passage-ways was an ingenious system of subways to house water and electrical services, and to convey coal to the many open fires throughout the hospital. As befitted any hospital of that era, the ward floors were 'of solid teak plank flooring in narrow widths, closely jointed, embedded in prepared pitch, and well run in with bees'-wax'.

By the time of the official opening on 13th May 1903, Edinburgh had a new Lord Provost, James Steel, who presided at the ceremony performed by King Edward VII. Immediately after the ceremony, King Edward conferred a baronetcy on Lord Provost Steel. The opening was a very grand affair with a processional route through Morningside, up Comiston Road and along the line of what is now Greenbank Drive. When Charles J. Smith was researching the district for Volume 2 of his *Historic South Edinburgh*, published in 1979, he interviewed several residents of Morningside who recalled the royal procession making its way out of town to the new Colinton Mains Hospital. By 1902 the estimated costs of the hospital had risen to £340,000, to serve Edinburgh's population of 330,000 – Dr Littlejohn's dream was about to come true for a little more than £1 per head.

Dr Claude Buchanan Ker was the first Medical Superintendent at the City Hospital, having transferred, with his staff, from the previous City Hospital near Infirmary Street, where he had been appointed Medical Superintendent in 1897. Besides diseases such as cholera and typhus, Dr Ker was an acknowledged expert in the containment and management of smallpox. From 1904, smallpox patients were accommodated in a

Their Majesties' Visit, May 1903. Opening of Colinton Mains Hospital.

The City Hospital, or Colinton Mains Hospital, was opened on 13th May 1903 by King Edward VII, in the presence of the Lord Provost, James Steel.

small timber-built hospital on the north-west corner of the new City Hospital site.

Dr Ker, supported by a small group of junior doctors, and Miss J. Thomas, the Matron, ran the new hospital with an iron rod. From the outset, notices posted on each ward reminded the staff that 'Any nurse guilty of neglect of, or cruelty to, a patient, practical joking, indecorum, insubordination, or who enters a ward or corridor other than her own without direct permission of Dr Ker, shall be liable to instant dismissal and loss of certificate'. The latter part of the directive was, of course, aimed at the prevention of cross infection between wards. Nurses, looking after scarlet fever patients on the east side of the hospital, wore pink uniforms, whilst the others wore blue. Even in the dining room staff were segregated, entering by different doors, receiving their food from separate serving hatches, and being screened from their colleagues by a glass partition. The spartan regime applied also in the nurses' home, with only one half-day off each week. Nurses working in the smallpox hospital, who had been re-vaccinated recently, were confined to the staff quarters of the smallpox hospital for six weeks or more, until the outbreak had subsided.

An aerial view of the City Hospital on the right, and the City Poorhouse on the left, looking east to the fields of Greenbank Farm. The steadings can just be seen in the top left-hand corner of the picture, c. 1931. *Courtesy of the Edinburgh City Archivist.*

In the early part of the twentieth century, and for many years thereafter, the City Hospital admitted a large number of patients suffering
from various forms of tuberculosis. Sir Robert Philip introduced very
effective management of the disease by bringing often terminally ill
people into hospital to limit the spread of infection in the community.
Initially, this practice earned the City Hospital an unenviably high
mortality rate, but sound procedures and good nursing eventually
brought respite to at least some of the patients. In the 1950s the battle
against tuberculosis was continued by Professor (later Sir) John Crofton
whose introduction of the triple drug treatment effectively controlled
the scourge of the disease in the population.

When the hospital first opened, more than half of the available beds
were assigned to scarlet fever patients. As the number of cases was
reduced over the years, there was a corresponding reduction in the
number of complications (which were often fatal) involving kidney
damage and infection of the bloodstream. The care of these patients
was, in itself, a dangerous occupation, several nurses dying of infections
such as scarlet fever, diphtheria, typhoid and tuberculosis. As infectious
diseases were slowly brought under control, and cholera and typhus
disappeared altogether, many hospital beds became vacant. This
allowed other medical and surgical specialties to make use of the empty
wards. These included: 1954, a cardio-thoracic unit at Pavilion 6; 1965,
the Ear, Nose and Throat Department; 1972, the Care of the Elderly
Unit; and 1991, when the Maxillo-facial surgeons joined the E.N.T.
Department.

When Sir John Crofton retired in 1978, the Respiratory Medicine
Unit continued under the leadership of Professor David Flenley until
his death in 1989. The emphasis of the Unit shifted from tuberculosis
to the treatment of chronic bronchitis and emphysema. Generous fund-
ing was obtained from the Rayne Foundation for the construction of
the Rayne Laboratory, and from the Salvesen Trust for research, first
by Professor Flenley, then by Professor Chris Haslett and their teams.
The Unit transferred to the Royal Infirmary in 1993.

In 1960 the Infectious Diseases Unit, later called the Regional
Infectious Diseases Unit (R.I.D.U.), was led by Dr James Murdoch in
succession to Dr Alec Joe, Medical Superintendent since 1937. Dr
Murdoch became internationally recognised for his research into new
antimicrobial drugs and the investigation of female urinary tract

A plethora of signs at the entrance to the City Hospital, in 1998, as it awaits imminent closure. *Photograph by Phyllis M. Cant.*

infection. The Unit absorbed the work of the Tropical Diseases Unit in 1972. On the retirement of Dr Murdoch in 1983 his place was taken by Dr Ray Brettle who made substantial progress on the emerging probems of HIV infection and AIDS, particularly in the Edinburgh area. Lothian Health Board and the Waverley Trust jointly funded the first purpose-built AIDS hospice in the United Kingdom, Milestone House, in the grounds of the hospital.

In addition to the clinical units, the X-ray Department and the various laboratories have contributed much to the reputation of the hospital. Before the Rayne Laboratory was built, a Respiratory Function Laboratory provided physiological measurements for patients with bronchial disorders, and the Bacteriology Department gave invaluable assistance to the clinicians. A Regional Virus Laboratory was established in 1970 as an expansion of the original Wellcome Laboratory opened in 1961, and the Scottish Mycobacterial Reference Laboratory transferred to the City Hospital from Mearnskirk Hospital in 1980.

No lack of direction here despite the announcement that the City Hospital is
scheduled for closure. *Photograph by Phyllis M. Cant.*

When the City Hospital opened in 1903 it was financed and controlled
by the Town Council. On the introduction of the National Health
Service in 1948 it came under the control of the South East Scotland
Regional Hospital Board but still remained part of the Royal Victoria
and Associated Hospitals Board of Management until the reorganisation
of the National Health Service in Scotland in 1974. After several further
managerial changes the City Hospital became part of the Royal Infirmary of Edinburgh N.H.S. Trust in 1993.

Despite the City Hospital's excellent contribution to the world of
medicine it will not see its centenary, as a decision has already been
taken to close the hospital. Many of the functions have already been
tranferred to other hospitals. The extensive site has been sold to Morrison Homes Ltd., who plan an innovative housing complex, retaining
most of the original buildings, erecting some new housing, and introducing new landscaping in keeping with the site.

The definitive history of the hospital has been researched by Dr James
A. Gray, Consultant Physician in Communicable Diseases in the

Regional Infectious Diseases Unit between 1969 and 1995, and is in the course of publication.

THE MERCHANTS OF EDINBURGH GOLF CLUB

The Merchants of Edinburgh Golf Club was established on Easter and Wester Craiglockhart Hill on 6th November 1907 when a group of 'merchants, clergymen, doctors, lawyers, journalists and others' decided to form the first club. In its first year, membership totalled 392 and the annual subscription was three guineas. Ben Sayers, the professional of North Berwick, selected the line of play for the 18-hole course, taking full advantage of the natural setting whilst minimising, as far as was practical, the distraction of too much hill climbing. The completed course, which totalled 4,118 yards over 77 acres, clearly won the approval of *Golf Illustrated* in October 1908: 'Altogether, the course is most admirably suited for the purpose for which it was acquired, viz., to enable the merchants of the city to enjoy their favourite game on reasonable terms, under the best conditions, and within easy access of their places of business'.

Since 1908 some fundamental changes have been made to the course layout. In 1925 the respective positions of the first and second halves of the course were reversed, and the opportunity was taken to recognise the members' improved skills by increasing the number of bunkers from 7 to 28. Six years later, the committee were obliged to make another change, this time from an unexpected direction. When the private road originally built to the City Poorhouse (now Glenlockhart Road) was opened up to the public, it created a major problem at the ring hole. Ominously numbered 13, it was played from the north slope of Wester Craiglockhart Hill *across* the road to a green on the *opposite* side. With the assistance of P. Robertson, the Braid Hills Professional, the line of the 13th hole was altered and the course redesigned at that point. A few years later, in 1934, five acres of ground were acquired to the west of the City Hospital, enabling the 5th, 6th and 7th holes to be repositioned. By 1941, however, part of the new ground was ploughed up to grow vegetables during the Second World War, and it was not until 1948 that the ground was reinstated. The present course is 4,889 yards long, par 65, over 82 acres.

The clubhouse, in the north-east corner of the course, is substantially

The members of the Provisional and Club Councils for 1907, 1908 and 1909 of the Merchants of Edinburgh Golf Club in 1909. Back Row: T. R. McIlwrick, D. Thompson, James Waugh, John Mackenzie (Treasurer). Middle Row: John Milne, J. Scott Marshall, W. A. Middleton, P. Waldie, Allan McGill, J. C. H. Balmain, William Alston. Seated: D. Reid, W. Brydon Hogg (Vice-Captain), William Lindsay (Captain), John Gibson, James Summers. Reclining: Alfred J. F. Mitchell (Secretary). *Courtesy of the Merchants of Edinburgh Golf Club.*

the original building, started in May 1908, completed in January 1909, and officially opened by Baillie Inches on 25th September 1909. The cost, at £1,300, was defrayed by loans and a system of £5 debentures offered to the members. The original verandah was enclosed in the 1960s. Internally the various facilities have been progressively extended over the years to include new locker rooms, a lounge, bar, dining room and committee room. In 1997 a decision was taken to have the old clubhouse demolished and new facilities built on the same site to be operational well before the club's centenary in 2007.

The Merchants, like any other club nearing its centenary, has hosted many formal and informal events, all carefully recorded in the minute books: 25.9.1909, at the opening of the course, an exhibition match was played by Ben Sayers of North Berwick and W. Binnie of Kinghorn; 1919, as part of Peace Celebration Week, the club entertained 850 members of the City Poorhouse to a dance and tea party; 1.9.1932, to commemorate the twenty-fifth anniversary of the club, an exhibition match was played by four Scottish Internationalists, J. B. Stevenson, E. A. McRuvie, K. C. Forbes and J. McLean; in 1957, at the Jubilee celebrations, an exhibition match was played by four leading lady golfers, Miss Janette Robertson, Miss Jessie Valentine, Miss Betty Singleton and Miss Jean Donald; and in 1982, at the seventy-fifth anniversary, an exhibition match was played between lady professionals Dale Reid of Ladybank, partnered by Joan Smith of Carnoustie, against Frank Rennie of Prestwick and Bobby Jamieson of Dunblane.

In the 1950s a small group of mainly young members at the Merchants formed Westermont, a small 'club within a club' to enable them to play competitively, away from their home course. This also allowed them to compete in the *Dispatch* Trophy which was not open to course-owning clubs: Westermont won the *Dispatch* Trophy in 1969 and 1989. Although the Merchants cannot compete directly in the *Dispatch* Trophy, it has its own wide range of cups and trophies, most of which are still played for. In this short synopsis of the club only a few are mentioned. The Club Championship has three divisions: Class A for which the Quaich was presented in 1910; Class B for which the Campbell Cormack Trophy was presented in 1923 by A. Campbell Cormack, a past captain of the club; and the Junior Championship Cup, presented in 1955 by the members. In addition, there are separate trophies for each of the Spring, Summer and Autumn Meetings, and many others including the William M. Herd Trophy, presented in 1978 by W. M. Herd of Christchurch, New Zealand for the New Year's Day Competition. The Ladies' Section has an equally varied list. The Ladies' Championship consists of: Silver, the Cruttenden Shield, presented by Mrs E. J. Cruttenden in 1925; and Bronze, the Clark Trophy, presented by Miss A. F. Clark in 1970. The Spring Meeting plays for the Skene Vase; the Summer Meeting plays for the Harriet Steven Thomson Trophy; and the Autumn meeting plays for the Graham Cup. Of the many others, perhaps the most innovative is the

In 1946 Alan F. D. MacGregor of the Merchants won the British Boys'
Championship at Bruntsfield Links Golfing Society against Donald Dunston of
Manchester, who had just beaten Peter Alliss in the Semi-Final.
Courtesy of the Merchants of Edinburgh Golf Club.

Grandmothers' Competition for which a cup was presented in 1976 by
Mrs J. Goulding.

Among the many members who have played at the Merchants, several
have reached national acclaim in the world of golf. The earliest was
undoubtedly Alfred J. F. Mitchell who became Irish Amateur Champion
in 1908, the year after the club was formed. Some years later, in 1946,
Alan F. D. MacGregor won the British Boys' Championship at Bruntsfield Links Golfing Society against Donald Dunston of Manchester, who
had just beaten Peter Alliss in the semi-final. Later, Alliss referred to
the event in his characteristic style: 'It all started in the British Boys'
Championship at Bruntsfield. The winner that year was A. F. D. Mac-
Gregor, a huge chap about six foot four inches who wore blue shorts
and had legs like telegraph poles'. In more recent years, Gavin Hastings,
of rugby fame, was a junior member from 1973 to 1979 and won the
inaugural Bert Bain Junior Singles in 1978. Two past captains of the
club have held high office outwith the Merchants: A. Lindsay Stewart
was president of the Lothians Golf Association in 1978 and president
of the Scottish Golf Union in 1991; and Ian R. Graham was president
of the Lothians Golf Association in 1995.

In the clubhouse a small permanent display of photographs commem-
orates the unique achievements of two past members, both of whom
were awarded the Victoria Cross. Lt. David Stuart McGregor of the
6th Battalion, The Royal Scots was posthumously awarded the Victoria
Cross for his bravery under fire on 22nd October 1918, near
Hoogemolen in Belgium. John Cruikshank, Royal Air Force Volunteer
Reserves, was awarded the Victoria Cross during the Second World
War as a pilot of a Catalina who flew his stricken aircraft, and crew,
from a position north-west of Norway to Sullom Voe, in Shetland,
despite having been critically injured by enemy fire.

The Merchants of Edinburgh Golf Club will celebrate its centenary
in 2007 when the full history of the club will be published. In the
meantime a new lease of the ground has been secured for a period of
99 years – almost to the time of the bicentenary. Over the years membership has increased from 516 in 1919 to 874 in 1997 which includes
the Junior Section and the Ladies' Section established in 1909. The
course record of 77, first set in 1908 by J. Dunlop, was gradually reduced
over the years. W. J. Jeffrey Jnr's 62 in 1974 remained unbeaten until
A. Helm returned a 59 in 1995. In 1938 the club considered, but rejected,

During the winter of 1982, when the Merchants of Edinburgh Golf Course was in the grip of a mini ice-age, the members turned their allegiance, temporarily, to the game of curling. *Courtesy of the Merchants of Edinburgh Golf Club.*

the idea of changing its name to Craiglockhart Golf Club. The Merchants of Edinburgh Golf Club has never had any formal association with the Company of Merchants of the City of Edinburgh, established in 1681. In 1998 the club captain was Douglas J. May Q.C., and the vice-captain was Douglas G. Naismith.

More detailed information on the history of the Merchants can be found in two publications, privately printed, namely, *Merchants of Edinburgh Golf Club 1907–1982* by Ian R. Graham, and *Golf on the Braid and Craiglockhart Hills*, 1991, by Jane George at Edinburgh University's School of Scottish Studies.

SOUTH MORNINGSIDE PRIMARY SCHOOL

South Morningside Primary School, in Comiston Road, was not built on the Lands of Greenbank, but its modern catchment area includes all of the streets of Greenbank. When the school was first built, 80% of its pupils came from houses north of Morningside Station. Over the years, however, the shift in population has meant that the school now draws many more pupils from areas to the south of the school.

The Education (Scotland) Act of 1872 made education compulsory, in Scotland, between the ages of 5 and 13. Central control was in the hands of the Scotch Education Board, in London, who implemented the provisions of the Act through a system of local School Boards. Fairly modest fees were payable to begin with but they were abolished in 1889. South Morningside School was opened in 1892 under the control of St Cuthbert's and Dean School Board, which was replaced by the Edinburgh School Board in 1895.

The school building was designed by the Board's architect, Robert Wilson, in a style very similar to other board schools throughout the city, including Castlehill, Torphichen Street, South Bridge and Sciennes. Although most of these buildings are still extant, many of them are no longer used for primary education. South Morningside, with its symmetrical façade and distinctive central lantern, was built of Hailes stone with red sandstone dressings, in 1891. In the spirit of the times, boys and girls were segregated in the playground area and they entered the school by separate doors. The classes were integrated but the boys sat at one side of the room and the girls at the other, separated by a wide passageway. Many of the classrooms were raked towards the back.

South Morningside School had two opening days: firstly on 5th September 1892 to admit the pupils; and then, more formally, on 3rd October 1892, to admit the dignitaries. On the day that the pupils were first admitted, the headmaster, John King, wrote in the School Log:

> 5 September 1892. This school was opened today at 9 o'clock when Mr Hew Morrison, Chairman, and Councillor Scott and Mr I. Sawers Mitchell, members of the School Board, and also a number of parents of the pupils, were present. The children all assembled in the Infant Room and after prayer by the Rev. Mr Howie, one of the parents, short addresses were given by Mr Morrison, Councillor Scott, Mr Mitchell, and the Headmaster. The Classes were then formed (each class comprising the pupils in one Standard), taken to their respective Rooms, and dismissed for the day. There were 344 pupils present. For the last few weeks attendance has been given at the school for the purpose of

The Old Schoolhouse in Morningside Road was closed when South Morningside School was opened in 1892. *Courtesy of Elizabeth McIlwrick.*

enrolment and altogether 522 names of intending pupils have been received.

Within the first few days 572 pupils had been enrolled, some attending school for the first time, but most coming from the old Morningside School in Morningside Road (now the Old School House), James Gillespie's in Gillespie Crescent, Gorgie Public School, and a host of small private schools.

The formal opening of the school took place on 3rd October 1892, attended by several dignitaries, including Professor David Masson, Professor of Rhetoric and English Literature at the University of Edinburgh, and Andrew Carnegie, the world-famous industrialist and philanthropist. Again, the headmaster recorded the event for posterity:

> Professor Masson formally opened the School today and in doing so gave an address in which he contrasted the elementary schools of 60 years ago with those of today. Mr Hew Morrison occupied the chair and in his speech related the circumstances under which the school was built and went on to remark on the satisfactory start the school had made. Mr Andrew Carnegie and Sir Thomas Clark also delivered short addresses. Over 300 parents and others presented themselves at the school but many failed to gain admission in consequence of the limited accommodation. Standards V and VI sang several songs and the Infants gave an exhibition which was much appreciated by those present. The remaining pupils were absent and the day was regarded as a school holiday.

From all accounts the school was popular from the outset, requiring a large extension, which was opened in 1898. Further space was gained from 1904 when pupils, who had passed the Qualifying Examination, left to go to Boroughmuir, George Watson's, Queen Street College and Heriot's.

When the school celebrated its centenary in 1992, its history was written by a group of parents and staff under the title *South Morningside Primary School: A Centenary History, 1892–1992*. It is an excellent amalgam of comment and anecdote in which the school log book entries are brought to life by a series of early photographs and contributions from former pupils and members of staff. An entry for 5th June 1893 indicates that even the headmaster can have a moment of mental aberration: 'Children in many cases do not concentrate their attention sufficiently on their own work while performing their written excercises [sic]'.

In the early part of the twentieth century, and well into the 1920s and 1930s, the health of school-children was a constant concern. According to a report in 1913 by the chief schools' medical officer, one child in twelve in Britain's primary schools suffered from disease or the effects of poor diet. It was not until 1924 that vaccination against infectious diseases was introduced into schools. Younger children especially suffered from recurring outbreaks of chicken pox, measles, mumps, scarlet fever and whooping cough. Other comparative data show how the practice of child employment decreased substantially between 1909 and 1930. In the 1909 sample, 138 children had some kind of employment (twice as many boys as girls) in a wide variety of businesses, but mainly dairies, bakers, stationers and grocers. By 1930 only 17 pupils were employed, all in the age group 11 to 13. During the 1930s the log books record a wide range of topics, some quite mundane, but others of national importance: 1931, a new piano arrives in school; 1935, 400 cherry trees planted in Braidburn Valley by 5,000 Guides, Rangers and Brownies to celebrate the Silver Jubilee of King George V and Queen Mary; 1938, gas masks issued and gas mask drill for all children.

The last item gave an ominous warning of what lay ahead. On 2nd September 1938 the school gymnasium was taken over for the storage of equipment in connection with air raid precautions, and in the following March workmen arrived to fit blackouts to all the windows and rooflights. Evacuation was imminent. On 25th August 1939 teachers were instructed over the national radio to return urgently to their schools to make preparations. A rehearsal was organised on Monday 28th August, followed by the full evacuation on Saturday 2nd September. Only 407 children out of a possible 1,006 presented themselves for 'transportation' to Aviemore, Boat of Garten and Nethy Bridge. Britain declared war on Germany at 11 a.m. on 3rd September 1939. As the school was closed, the pupils who had remained in Edinburgh were taught in small groups in the local church halls, and in private houses in and around Morningside Road and Greenbank. When the anticipated widespread air raids did not occur, many evacuees drifted back to Edinburgh. Air raid shelters were erected in the playground and the school reopened on a double-shift basis. By February 1941 the average school roll was 399. Throughout the war years there were constant interruptions in the teaching timetable, chronic shortages of equipment and materials, and, of course, food rationing which continued for some years after the end of the Second World War in 1945.

Forbes Macgregor became headmaster of South Morningside School in 1951 and held the position until his retirement in 1965. The immediate post-war years were dominated by the problems of inadequate school buildings, many of which had deteriorated and/or had become too small for the rising number of schoolchildren. South Morningside School was no exception. After several abortive plans for a new school building, Comiston Annexe was opened on 14th April 1969, and became a separate school in 1971 with its own headmaster and infant mistress. Mr Macgregor was succeeded by Mr John Sloss until he transferred to Craiglockhart Primary School in 1971. When the new headmaster, Mr George Mutch, took up his appointment in August 1971 the school roll was a manageable 585, much reduced from earlier years by the opening of Comiston School. Within a few years, however, lack of accommodation was again a problem, solved this time by using part of the Upper Hall as a classroom, and Cluny Centre for Physical Education lessons. Between November 1975 and April 1976 most classes were transferred to North Merchiston School to allow extensive work to be undertaken at South Morningside for the eradication of dry rot.

The present headteacher, Mrs Jeanette Perry, came to South Morningside School in October 1982. In her contribution to *South Morningside Primary School: A Centenary History, 1892–1992*, Mrs Perry recalls being very aware, when she first arrived, of the hustle and bustle of hundreds of children making their way up and down the double staircase in the centre of the building. It was already the age of technology in which computers and videos had become standard equipment, financed, in part, by donations from the Parent Teacher Association Committee. Following government legislation, the first South Morningside Primary School Board was formed in October 1989 with five parent representatives, two members of staff and two co-opted members. The main purpose of the School Board was, and still is, to improve communication between the education authority, the school and the parents. Among its many duties are: to participate in the selection of promoted staff; to approve the headteacher's plan for the

South Morningside Primary School, in Comiston Road, was designed by Robert
Wilson, architect to the Edinburgh School Board, and built of Hailes stone with
red sandstone dressings, in 1891. The formal opening was on 3rd October 1892.
Photograph by Phyllis M. Cant.

purchase of books and materials; and to decide arrangements for the
use of the school building outwith school hours.

At the end of 1991 the school held preparatory events for the centenary in the following year. In October 1991 the original school bell was
re-hung in the tower, to be used on special occasions, and the school's
centenary history, *South Morningside Primary School: A Centenary
History, 1892–1992* was published in November 1991. During 1992
commemorative tea-towels, T-shirts and mugs were produced, a mural
was painted on the playground wall, and trees were planted in the
playground. There were parties and concerts, leading up to the grand
finale in September 1992 when all the pupils and staff dressed in Victorian clothes, and paraded down to the bottom of Comiston Road,
round into Braid Road, and back along Braidburn Terrace for a special

service at Greenbank Parish Church, presided over by the school chaplain, the Rev. Ian G. Scott

Such then is the story of Greenbank, a district which came to prominence in the 1930s when the building of bungalow developments was popular in Edinburgh. The origin of the name 'Greenbank', however, dates from at least the early seventeenth century as an alternative name for Over Plewlands of Braid. It is an area with greater historical associations than is evident at first glance. This is especially so when the study extends to the wider boundaries of the original Lands of Greenbank, and their juxtaposition with neighbouring estates such as Braid, Comiston and Craiglockhart. The district has seen many changes over the centuries and no doubt will continue to see more in the future.

Suggestions for Further Reading

Author	Title	Date of Publication
Colson, James	*The Edinburgh & District Water Supply*	1890
Dunlop, Rev. A. Ian	*The Kirks of Edinburgh*	1988
Edinburgh Corporation	*The Water Supply of Edinburgh*	Not dated
Gifford, John, McWilliam, Colin & Walker, David	*The Buildings of Scotland – Edinburgh*	1984
Grant, James	*Old and New Edinburgh*	1882
Harris, Stuart	*The Place Names of Edinburgh*	1996
Lewis, David	*Edinburgh Water Supply*	1908
Mackay, Rev. Donald G.M.	*The Story of Greenbank*	1990
Mullay, Sandy	*The Edinburgh Encyclopaedia*	1996
Nimmo, Ian	*Edinburgh's Green Heritage*	1996
Smith, Charles J.	*Historic South Edinburgh* Four volumes	1978 1979 1986 1988
Smith, Charles J.	*South Edinburgh in Pictures*	1989
Smith, Charles J.	*Morningside*	1992
South Morningside Primary School	*A Centenary History, 1892–1992*	1992
Various	*The Book of the Old Edinburgh Club*	1908 to date
Warrender, Margaret	*Walks near Edinburgh*	1895

Index

Note: page references in *italics* refer to illustrations